Taunton's

ALL NEW Decorating

IDEA BOOK

Taunton's

ALL NEW Decorating

IDEA BOOK

HEATHER J. PAPER

The Taunton Press

The Taunton Press, Inc.
63 South Main Street, PO Box 5506
Newtown, CT 06470-5506
e-mail: tp@taunton.com

Editor: Christina Glennon
Copy editor: Diane Sinitsky
Jacket/Cover design: Kimberly Adis
Interior design: Kimberly Adis
Layout: David Giammattei
Illustrators: Jean Tuttle
Photo editor: Erin Giunta
Cover Photographer: Main Front Cover: Brian Vanden Brink; Front Cover Top: Mark Lohman; Front Cover Bottom: Stacy Bass; Back Cover: Clockwise from Top: Ryann Ford; David Duncan Livingston; Ken Gutmaker; Ryann Ford
Main cover photo designer credit: Architect/Builder: Polhemus Savery Dasilva; Interior Designer: Denise Maurer Interiors of Troy, NY, Painting by David Witbeck/Cove Gallery

Library of Congress Cataloging-in-Publication Data

Paper, Heather J.
 All new decorating idea book / Heather J. Paper.
     pages cm
 Summary: "This book includes ideas for freshening up a tired look, small-scale renovations, and larger transformations"-- Provided by publisher.
 ISBN 978-1-62710-116-5 (paperback)
1. Interior decoration. I. Title.
 NK2115.P2783 2014
 747--dc23
                                        2014025180

Printed in the United States of America
10 9 8 7 6 5 4 3 2 1

# acknowledgments

UPON ENTERING COLLEGE, I knew that I wouldn't be pursuing a career in the field of teaching. (I simply didn't have the patience, or so I told myself.) Instead, I collected degrees in journalism and interior design, and I have since written on every imaginable decorating topic.

Ironically, all these years later, teaching is one of the things I love most. I thoroughly enjoy explaining the whys and wherefores of everything from smart floor plans to successful color schemes. And that's why writing this particular book has been a pure pleasure.

My sincere thanks go to Peter Chapman and Christina Glennon at The Taunton Press, who showed great faith in me every step of the way. Thanks, too, to Erin Giunta for keeping such a massive number of photographs organized. Additionally, many thanks go to Carolyn Mandarano; I continue to benefit from the mentoring she's provided.

But the team that's truly responsible for this book includes numerous others, as well. Photographers who provided top-notch images for this book. Designers who've inspired my writing for years. Family members who have been there through thick and thin, encouraging all of my writing endeavors. And friends that I can count on night or day, among them Deb Baker, Colleen Summers, Shirley Van Zante, and—last but not least—Victoria Lane. The sound of her laughter alone can chase away the worst case of writer's block.

Finally, I want to thank my husband, Russ, whose love and support go back more than 25 years. His believing in me, unwaveringly, means more than he will ever know—and has made me the writer I am today.

# contents

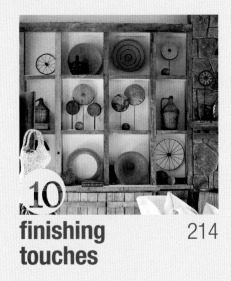

# introduction

AVING A BACKGROUND IN INTERIOR design has its advantages—and some disadvantages, too. I can't begin to count the number of times I've heard, "Your house must be gorgeous; I can't let you see mine!" I suspect I've lost out on more than one dinner invitation that way.

But here's the reality: While it's true that I've been schooled in basic design concepts, my house isn't all that different from yours. It's filled with furnishings in my preferred style

(eclectic) and colors that are comfortable to me (blues, greens, and all manner of soothing hues). Plus, it's a reflection of my personality (a collection of dog portraiture gives me away as a fan of man's best friend).

Those three elements—style, color, and personal touches—are the basic foundation of any well-designed room. And you probably have a good idea of your own preferences. But whether you're self-assured or a bit unsettled about the decorating process, this

book is certain to take you to the next level. It's filled with information and inspiration, providing guidance for everything from smart room arrangements and color combinations to selecting accessories.

Some ideas presented within these pages may have never occurred to you, while others might solidify those of your own. But that's in keeping with the process. There is no one right solution; rooms are ever evolving, as tastes and family dynamics change. Through

it all, keep this book close at hand. There are plenty of decorating lessons to be learned, for the novice or the most seasoned decorator.

Take it from me. Even as a professional in this field, the *All New Decorating Idea Book* is precisely the kind of publication I look to for inspiration of my own.

# style

● ● ●

HOME. IT'S A HAVEN AMIDST THE HUSTLE AND BUSTLE OF TODAY'S hurry-up world. From the moment you get up and head to the kitchen for breakfast to the time you retire to the bedroom at the end of the day, it wraps you in comfort and warmth—not only because it's a safe place to land but also because it reflects your personal style.

Surrounding yourself with familiar and favorite things is not only pleasing to look at but also uplifting. What's more, those same things "introduce" you to guests as they walk through the front door, offering a clue to your style persona. Canvas-slipcovered seating speaks to a casual lifestyle, while fine antiques signal a traditionalist. Likewise, cutting-edge contemporary interiors are often preferred by those who live life on the edge.

That's not to say that the home isn't hardworking. It's often the preferred place to gather with family and friends. You'll find some owners whipping up meals in their well-equipped kitchens, then serving epicurean feasts in formal dining rooms.

**Everything about this room speaks to a casual, laid-back lifestyle. A stacked-stone fireplace sets the tone, inspiring a soothing neutral color scheme that's played out in everything from wall and floor coverings to seating pieces upholstered in tough-as-nails fabrics that can take daily wear.**

Meanwhile, others are entertaining informally, with guests gathered in the family room around a flat-screen TV. Home offices are often a priority, as well, whether solely intended for paying monthly bills or dedicated to a home-based business. But the beauty of it is that you can have it all, throughout the house marrying fashion and function, style with servability.

# selecting a style

● ● ● PERHAPS YOU HAVE A CLEAR VISION OF your personal style, one that best suits your family's wants and needs. If not, start by considering whether your family tends to live formally or if they are completely laid back; your preference will surely impact the way you decorate your home. So, too, will your preferences in furniture styles. Are you most at home in a traditional setting, complete with family heirlooms? Or do you find yourself preferring a city loft filled with contemporary pieces?

If you're still undecided about your style, try this simple exercise: Thumb through magazines—and this book—looking for rooms that you find particularly appealing; there are sure to be some common aspects that will give you a sense of where to start. It may be a certain type of sofa, a particular color, or simply the feeling you get from the room. Don't be surprised, either, if you find that you like a variety of design styles; an eclectic approach can be one of the best ways to put your personal stamp on a room. As long as the disparate styles all have clean, classic forms, they'll work together beautifully.

**ABOVE** A quick glimpse of this living room not only offers a clue to the owners' style preference— purely modern—but literally hints to its location near sandy dunes. Those dunes may have even inspired the color of the sofa, complemented here by bright pops of turquoise and orange.

**RIGHT** Contemporary style need not be limited to sharp edges and cool metal surfaces. In this dining area, the table and chairs are contemporary in style but, because they're made of wood, bring a warm feeling to the room.

**FACING PAGE** A canopy treatment at the head of this bed immediately gives the room a sense of traditional style, carried out further by the classic seating pieces, chandelier, and even the art and accessories.

# translating ideas

● ● ● TO A LARGE DEGREE, TRANSLATING IDEAS is what decorating is all about. You may be inspired by a beautiful room in a magazine, but to make it work for your family there may need to be some tweaks along the way. Once you've honed in on a particular style, for instance, give some thought to your family's specific needs. Do you have a house full of children and pets? If so, that linen-covered wing chair you love should probably be upholstered in chenille or some other tough-as-nails fabric instead. Does your family enjoy watching TV together? In lieu of a standard-size sofa, consider an L-shaped sectional that can accommodate everyone.

You may find, too, that something you have your heart set on is beyond your budget. But you can translate the look to suit your budget and your sense of style. Maybe you have your eye on a media center that's beyond your price range. Keep in mind that you can find similar designs in discount retail stores and even home centers. Yearning for a stone floor in your kitchen? Many of today's ceramic tiles are great pretenders, replicating the look at a fraction of the price and providing easier-care options. The bottom line is this: Start by deciding on the look you want, then translate the idea to suit *your* color scheme, *your* lifestyle, and *your* budget.

**BELOW Though generous in size, a pair of sofas in this contemporary living room doesn't take up much visual space; the neutral upholstery blends quietly into the similar hues of the surroundings. At the same time, the color choice allows a navy blue chair to stand out as a statement piece.**

An abundance of golds and browns wrap this master bedroom in a layer of warmth. Though the room's roots are firmly embedded in country style, select accents—like the driftwood lamp and whimsical art over the bed—give the space a subtle contemporary twist.

**ABOVE** In a ranch-style home with no separate foyer, the owners created the feeling of one. A small throw rug establishes the sense of a hallway, while a nearby console table provides a place to put keys and mail.

**RIGHT** Proving that even a minimal space can have maximum style, this home office area makes the most of every square inch. Even a side wall is coated with chalkboard paint to serve as a handy message board.

# decorating decisions

● ● ● AT THE SAME TIME YOU'RE CONSIDERING your furnishings, it's important to take into account practical matters. Be sure, for instance, that the tall cupboard you admire will not only fit in your room but will also fit through the front door. Just as a carpenter's rule of thumb is to "measure twice, cut once," a similar philosophy applies to furniture shopping: Measure twice, buy once—and don't go shopping without a tape measure. The soaring ceilings that you typically find in furniture stores often make pieces seem smaller than their actual size. In fact, it's a good idea to create a notebook to take with you on shopping trips, complete with your room's dimensions as well as any samples of fabrics, flooring, and wall coverings that are already in place.

Think, too, beyond conventional furniture stores. Search your own basement or attic: Is there a long-forgotten chair or chest that, with a new fabric or finish, could be recycled right back into use? Likewise, search out online sites, antiques stores, and salvage shops. There's no telling when you might stumble across that perfect piece and save a few dollars in the process.

A vintage buffet fits perfectly into this dining room's niche, its surface—as well as the art—illuminated by a recessed light. Tucking the storage piece into the niche allows for easier traffic flow around the nearby table, too.

**FACING PAGE TOP**
Calling on a variety of resources for a room's furnishings can make it more visually interesting. Once upholstery pieces are selected, for instance, team them with tables that are brand new as well as reclaimed and with fine antiques as well as flea-market finds.

**FACING PAGE BOTTOM LEFT**
Creativity overtakes this contemporary home office. What was once a standard double closet has been outfitted with price-wise shelves and file cabinets, the background then painted a bright orange to echo the color of the tuck-away stool. A rolling garage-style door can be pulled down to quickly hide the clutter.

**ABOVE** Thinking outside the box can stretch your decorating dollar and add an extra element of personal style at the same time. In this bedroom, an oversize target takes the place of a conventional headboard, perhaps revealing the resident's penchant for archery?

# sharpening your vision

● ● ● ONCE YOU'VE SELECTED THE MAJOR PIECES of furniture and settled on a color scheme, start from the outside of the room and work in. Using the patterns and colors in upholstered pieces as inspiration, select window and wall coverings. Then, shift your focus to the floor. Make sure that everything is showcased with the right lighting. And, finally, choose accessories that are not only decorative but also speak to your interests, your travels, and your personality.

It's easier than ever to find decorating information and inspiration, not only in this book but also by surfing the Web. And with that increased knowledge comes greater confidence. When it comes to decorating, there are guidelines but no real right or wrong approaches. In the end, it all comes down to individual style.

Dramatic pops of black provide continuity in this living room, leading the eye around the room from a pair of armchairs to zebra-patterned stools to black-shaded lamps and even black-framed artwork.

**ABOVE** Cottage style is all about simplicity, played out beautifully in this bedroom. An unpretentious taupe-and-white scheme is the perfect backdrop for equally humble elements like swag curtains, a rush-seated bench, even a headboard with a dainty scalloped edge.

**LEFT** Whether you live in the West or wish that you did, the right furnishings can create the feeling. In this family room, built-in banquette seating is decked out in colorful blankets and pillows. Better yet, because the seats are twin-size mattresses, they can accommodate overnight guests.

**LEFT** In this modern living/dining area, wall treatments visually separate the two; wood paneling defines the living room, while painted walls do the same in the dining space. The neutral colors of both clear the way, too, for pops of color in the furnishings, in the sofa and area rug, as well as in the nearby dining chairs.

# color

• • •

YOU MAY NOT EVEN BE AWARE OF IT, BUT COLOR IMPACTS YOU EVERY day. Imagine yourself sitting on a beach, watching the sea wash upon the sand. The cool hue of the water conveys a refreshing and relaxing feeling. Likewise, while sitting on that same beach, imagine the sun shining brightly—and the warming effect that it has.

But if color is influential in everyday life, it's even more so in the home, where you're surrounded by the same influences day after day. In no time at all, you come to associate a soothing blue bedroom with a calming retreat at the end of each day, a bright yellow kitchen with a cheery space in which to start the next.

There are, however, no longer any hard-and-fast rules for colors in certain spaces. Nurseries aren't restricted to pastels any more than libraries are to hunter green. Instead, it's more important to establish a color scheme that *you're* comfortable with. (Here's a hint: If you're comfortable wearing a particular color, you'll probably be comfortable living with it, too.) And, even then, the tints and shades you choose can play an important role in expressing your personal style. In a traditional residence,

**Blue is one of the best color choices in a bedroom; the color is restful and relaxing. The abundance of warm brown walls and window shades, though, keep the cool hue from turning cold.**

for instance, a pink nursery may be decked out in soft, pastel shades, while in more contemporary quarters, that pink may take on an intense, vibrant quality. And in a country-style scheme, it might shift to a rose-colored hue. In the end, it all comes down to comfort—from a visual point of view.

# picking a palette

● ● ● PICKING A ROOM'S COLOR PALETTE CAN be intimidating. After all, you have more than the colors of the rainbow to choose from; there are *all* those tints and shades in between the primary hues. Need proof? Try going to the paint store and simply asking for "white." You'll find an entire collection of whites to choose from, ranging from those that have a warm, cream-colored cast to cool versions that have a frosty air.

To make color decisions less daunting, look around your room for some clues. Is there a favorite work of art that will be the focal point of the room? Or, perhaps, an heirloom rug? If so, use that focal-point object as inspiration, pulling colors out of it to spread around the room. On the other hand, if you're starting from scratch, you might begin with your favorite color, then build on it just as you would a fashion ensemble. Creating a well-dressed home is, after all, no different.

**A brilliant red-orange—found in the armchair, bedside chests, and even the lamps—could have been overstimulating were it not for the soothing greens and neutral hues seen throughout the rest of the room.**

**LEFT** A treasured collection of blue-and-white ware inspired the scheme in this breakfast nook. It's echoed, in fact, quite literally, as the chairs' upholstery also features images of blue-and-white.

**BELOW** Chartreuse walls—both painted and papered—are appropriately contemporary for this kitchen, the vibrant color kept in check with an abundance of white cabinetry, counter stools, and an overhead lamp.

Inspired by a predominant work of art, the color scheme is solidly anchored by matching chocolate brown sofas, accented with a throw and decorative pillows in shades of orange and red. Because the rest of the room is decked out in creamy colors, the colorful furnishings stand out more prominently.

# •color combinations

When it comes to color combinations, there are definite classics. Blue-and-white, for instance, is a traditional favorite. But, to give blue a contemporary edge, pair it with bright lemon yellow or lime green. Or, for a country-style room, how about a denim blue hue complemented by the burnt orange typically found in the topstitching of jeans?

If you need inspiration for your own color combos, look no further than Mother Nature herself—the spring green of leaves with the browns of tree bark or the variegated shades of blue as you look from the water's edge out to sea. Many of today's manufacturers have made mixing colors a snap, too. Fabrics, for instance, often come in precoordinated collections that take the guesswork out of combining colors and patterns.

A mouth-watering chocolate brown wraps the walls of this family room and is repeated on the sofa and chair. The splashes of citrus, though, are what add excitement to the scheme, found in the lime green bench and throw pillows as well as assorted tangerine accents.

# CONTROLLING A ROOM'S TEMPERATURE

t o raise the temperature of a space, look to more than the thermostat. Color can be one of your best allies if you want to change the temperature of a room. Do you have a north-facing room, with limited sunlight, that seems to have an ever-present chill? Add a generous dose of a warm hue on the walls—red, orange, or yellow—to visually turn up the heat. Likewise, if your room is south-facing and gets plentiful sunshine, lower the visual temperature by wrapping it in a cool tone—blue, green, or purple.

The gold-painted walls and ceiling of this family room provide as much visual warmth as the fireplace does.

**TOP LEFT** The colors found in a contemporary work of art leap off the canvas in this bedroom, spreading a refreshing feeling throughout. Cool shades of yellow-green take the lead, warmed to just the right degree by touches of orange in the slipper chair and bed linens.

**LEFT** This living room puts a fresh spin on a timeless blue-and-white color scheme. Though many of the elements are traditional—like the sofa and pair of Fu Dogs behind it—the armchair's blue-and-white pattern has a contemporary feeling, as does the pair of lamps with see-through glass bases.

Blue, a nearly perfect partner for any color, teams up here with a rich brown. When considering color schemes, look to nature; this one, for instance, reflects the varied browns of tree bark against a pale blue sky.

## red and green: variations on a scheme

When using the most intense shades of color, a little bit goes a long way. The bright green frames of the chairs are kept in check by the neutral tones of the walls, the table, even the hardwood floor. Likewise, a pop of red in nearby artwork is neutralized by its white backdrop.

**TOP** Splashes of ruby red and jade green transform this powder room into a jewel box of a space, with the dramatic shapes and patterns of the sink and mosaic tile further upping the dramatic impact.

**ABOVE** The striped inset on this upholstered headboard inspired the red-and-green scheme in this bedroom. The soothing green hues of the walls, bed linens, and lampshade are punctuated with just a touch of the more powerful fuchsia.

# setting the mood

● ● ● THE MOOD-SETTING CAPABILITIES OF COLOR can be powerful. A bright tangerine exudes excitement, while a soft lavender is inevitably soothing. In fact, every color of the rainbow conveys some kind of mood. But, even within a single hue, various tints and shades can have completely different effects. A bold kelly green, for instance, can have a contemporary feeling, while a soft mint is typically more quiet and reserved.

Before putting your room in a particular mood, give careful thought to how the space will be used. Is it for working or resting? One requires energetic colors, while the other calls for more soothing hues. Is it public or private? For the former, you might want to use hues that will make most guests comfortable; bright colors, for instance, create a cheerful feeling. In private quarters, however, you can make more of a personal statement. The sky's the limit!

**Creating a soothing atmosphere conducive to sleep, this master bedroom is swathed in neutral hues running the gamut from soft cream to deep brown. While the quiet scheme is monochromatic, a variety of textures throughout keep it from becoming tiring.**

# ADD PATTERN

Sometimes, especially in a small space, an overall pattern can overwhelm a room. But that doesn't mean that you have to give up the idea completely. A feature wall can provide a room with an instant focal point. Artistic murals are one option; you'll find murals that feature everything from larger-than-life rose blossoms to whimsical animals that are perfect for kids' rooms. Or opt for an eye-popping graphic pattern. You can paint it directly on the wall or go for more instant gratification by applying some of today's colorful wall decals. They can be positioned—and repositioned—as often as you like and removed without a trace when you're ready to move on.

To create a graphic pattern like the one in this playroom, you need nothing more than painter's tape and the paint colors of your choice. Play with your pattern on graph paper first, using colored pencils or markers; then, simply translate the look to your wall.

**TOP** Energizing colors like the tangerine in this wallpaper can be a good choice for dining rooms as they can stimulate conversation. Pale blue chairs provide a good balance here, their restful hue keeping diners relaxed at the same time.

**LEFT** On the cool side of the color spectrum, blue has an inherently refreshing feeling. The color is perfectly suited for this screen porch, where laid-back living is the top priority.

# •living

Living and dining rooms are the most public spaces in any home. They're where you entertain family and friends, be it small get-togethers or large reunions. Neutrals are comforting to almost everyone, from shades of cream and beige to bold black and white—even certain shades of green.

But don't rule out the possibility of more colorful hues. Pale pinks and peaches (sometimes referred to as "cosmetic colors" because, like makeup, they complement the skin tones of those in the room) can be good choices in formal living rooms. Likewise, a deep red can work well in a dining room; this passionate, powerful hue stimulates conversation as well as the appetite.

**ABOVE** A subdued color scheme—like this pale gray-and-white example inspired by the area rug—is conducive to quiet candlelight dinners, inviting guests to linger just a little longer over a meal.

**RIGHT** At the end of a long day, a family room that's restful and relaxing can be a welcome retreat. This one sets the tone with soothing neutral hues, played out in generous doses of cream colors in seating pieces and wall trim, and punctuated with equally tranquil patterns.

**LEFT** Crimson red, a high-energy color, is well suited to eating areas where lively conversation is the norm. Coupled here with bright white furnishings and trim, the color seems even more brilliant by contrast.

**BELOW** A slight twist on a primary-color scheme makes this living room convivial. In lieu of the more expected red, a cheery orange teams up with shades of blue and yellow, resulting in a spirited space to welcome guests.

# • working

Certain colors are restful and relaxing, but those aren't the ones best suited for working spaces. Think about it: It's ill-advised to nod off during a conference call in your home office and downright dangerous to fall asleep while stirring a pot on the kitchen stove. Instead, opt for hues that are energizing, ones that will enliven the atmosphere. Good choices are shades that are intense in value, such as lemon yellow and cherry red or—if you're courageous with color—lime green, even citrus orange. By the same token, contrasting tones can be stimulating, even something as simple as black, or any vivid color, coupled with white.

**ABOVE** No longer limited to "safe" neutral hues, everyday appliances can provide a pop of color in a room. This crimson washer and dryer lend warmth to a room that otherwise—given its abundance of white—might have seemed cold.

**LEFT** Invigorating colors like this fuchsia are appropriate in a home office in order to keep the energy level high. There can, however, be too much of a good thing; here, the bright pink is balanced by plenty of white.

**FACING PAGE** Evidence that you don't need an abundance of color to make a big impact, this kitchen features an eye-catching element in the form of a subway-tiled backsplash in a palette punctuated by fresh-as-a-breeze turquoise and sunny orange.

# • sleeping

Cool colors—blue, green, and purple—are soothing by nature, particularly in subdued hues. For that matter, neutrals are soothing, too. But that's by no means the extent of shades that can create an appropriately relaxing atmosphere in the bedroom. Consider pastels, for instance. If they're apropos in a baby's nursery, why not in a grown-up's retreat, too? Perhaps not juvenile pinks and blues but, instead, more sophisticated shades of peach and lavender? On the other hand, colors such as golden yellow and rosy pink can blanket a bedroom with an extra layer of warmth. In short, choose any color that's comforting to you, and then take it to its most relaxing level.

**FACING PAGE TOP** The simplicity of this black-and-white color scheme is what makes it soothing. By bringing the black ceiling color down a few inches onto the walls, the height of the room appears lower and makes the space cozier at the same time.

**FACING PAGE BOTTOM** Limiting colors to one or two—plus a neutral—can keep a bedroom appropriately calm. In this boy's room, black and blue team up with a crisp white; because all three are used in similar amounts, the result is beautifully balanced.

**ABOVE** The warm gold tones used throughout this bedroom—in the bed linens, curtains, and the woven shades—add an extra layer of heat. Additionally, the regal color complements the warm wood finishes of the four-poster bed and bedside tables.

# incorporating color

● ● ● THERE'S VIRTUALLY NO END TO THE NUMBER of ways that color can be incorporated into a room. You may, for instance, choose to use your room as a canvas, wrapping the walls in white or another pale neutral and doing the same with the major pieces of furniture. Then, add accent colors in rugs, window treatments, and decorative pillows—changing them just as often as the mood strikes. Or take the next step and keep neutral hues on the wall but add color in the form of a sofa and chairs.

If you have a passion for color, you may opt to drench a room from floor to ceiling, painting the walls as well as the ceiling. Or you might wrap a room with an eye-popping pattern. It all depends on your personal comfort level with color. One thing's for sure, though: As your passion for color grows, your confidence level will, too.

ABOVE A blue lacquered finish on the wall, storage shelves, and drawers—even the nearby piano—gives this space a childlike exuberance, perfectly appropriate for an area dedicated to children's activities and accomplishments.

LEFT A decorative pillow provided the springboard for this bedroom's color scheme. The predominant linen, orange, and fuchsia hues found in the pillow's pattern are not only echoed throughout the room but used in the same proportions, too.

# •furniture

It may be a floral-strewn sofa. Or a paisley-covered chair. Even a brown leather ottoman does its part to bring color into a room via furniture. In fact, a favorite piece, whether it's a new purchase or something that's been in the family for years, can be the perfect springboard for an entire color scheme. Just be sure to balance the hues throughout the room. From that floral-strewn sofa, for instance, you may want to pull out the green accent color of the leaves, using it liberally in window treatments or floor coverings. Or offset it with generous doses of white. If, however, your focal point piece is a bright red sofa or server, repeat the hue sparingly—or not at all—so it will rightly retain the spotlight.

A red lacquered buffet and a red modern chair stand out in this living room like Technicolor elements of an otherwise black-and-white film, their silhouettes sharply defined by the contrast.

**ABOVE** An all-white surround makes this room's colorful furniture stand out more prominently. A solid blue sofa anchors the seating group, facing off against a pair of slipper chairs that—due to their small scale—require a more delicate pattern. Two armchairs, meanwhile, echo the blue-and-white hues while adding a touch of yellow for warmth.

**RIGHT** A basket-weave plaid headboard served as the starting point for this room's color scheme. The prevailing lime green reappears in window treatments as well as in the dust skirt, the solid color providing the visual weight needed to balance the size of the bed.

Using a single pattern eliminates the challenge of mix-and-match prints. A black-and-white toile is showcased in this bedroom, appearing not only in the window treatments but also in the headboard, bed skirt, and armchair. The complex pattern is kept in check by solid-color surfaces throughout the rest of the room.

# • windows and walls

If you're gradually building your color confidence, one of the best ways to infuse a room with color is with painted walls. Not only is the expense minimal but, if and when you tire of the effect, you can paint right over them. Likewise, colorful curtains at the windows— even simple sheers—can add an instant dose of color and are easy on the budget. It takes a little more color conviction to cover walls with a bright, retro-patterned wallpaper or hang ornate draperies along a window wall. The return, however, is well worth it. Not only will you infuse the room with color, but you'll inject plenty of personality, too.

**ABOVE** Because the window treatment is the only patterned element in this home office, it's the first thing that grabs your attention in the room. Leading the eye from floor to ceiling, it creates a greater sense of height, too.

**TOP** A wide-striped painted wall establishes the pink-and-white color scheme in this playroom. Although the pinks in the wall covering and upholstered chair—even the storage bins—don't match exactly, they do blend, which can be easier on the eye.

**RIGHT** A single wall decked out in sparkling green glass tile gives a tucked-away alcove more importance. The combination of color and pattern gives it focal-point status, while the cool hue is appropriately refreshing for a bath.

**ABOVE** A multicolored graphic wallpaper wraps this reading alcove, further intensifying its cozy feeling. Built-in bookshelves on opposite walls pull out mint green and ruby red colors, respectively, keeping the whimsical factor high.

**RIGHT** Paint is one of the fastest—and least expensive—ways to add color. The lime green walls of this bathroom create a refreshing feeling now but, if the mood strikes, could be repainted in a day.

more about...

# CHOOSING
# A PAINT COLOR

t oo often, a room's paint color is chosen from nothing more than a small strip from a fan deck. And, not surprisingly, the results can be disappointing. Perhaps your chosen hue looks too light, too dark, too yellow, too blue. The fact is, the same paint color can change dramatically depending on how much—and what kind of—light it gets. Is your room awash in natural light? Or do you only use it at night, when it's illuminated with lamps and overhead fixtures?

To better pinpoint the right color for your room, it pays to do some homework first. Most paint companies offer sample-size cans that contain a few ounces, just enough to paint a small area. Go to your local home center and purchase a 2-ft. by 2-ft. piece of drywall. Take it home and paint your color choice on the drywall, then prop the painted piece against one wall of the room, studying it at different times of the day. Be sure to move the piece from wall to wall, too, examining each placement for its effect. If this sounds too involved, look for the poster-size paint chips that some companies offer. These simply adhere to the wall and can be reused without marring the wall itself.

**ABOVE** Cool hues—blues, greens, and purples—are inherently soothing, making them a good choice for restful bedrooms. This one is drenched in a relaxing turquoise, with warm pink accents keeping it from being too cold.

# •floors and ceilings

In the past, floors and ceilings have typically been relegated to "safe" neutral hues. Floors were limited to go-with-anything cream-colored carpet, black-and-white tiles, and brown hardwood planks, while ceilings, more often than not, were simply left white.

That's all changed, however, as more homeowners see these large expanses of space as prime opportunities to bring color into a room. Neutral floorings have been replaced with brilliant carpet and ceramic tiles, even vivid forms of rubber and linoleum. And area rug options have never been more varied, nor affordable. Meanwhile, ceilings are—more and more—being treated like a "fifth wall," with just as much pattern and panache as their vertical counterparts.

**ABOVE** There's no need for the ceiling to get the short shrift; think of it as the "fifth wall." In this dining room, the ceiling is the focal point, thanks to an eye-catching paisley pattern that ties together the chocolate brown walls and bright white trim.

**ABOVE** Taking a color cue from the nearby area rug, stair risers in this back entry are painted spring green. The soft shade leads the eye right up the steps, giving importance to an oft-overlooked surface.

**RIGHT** A denim-colored carpet underscores this boy's room, grounding the all-white walls and ceiling. Its subtle plaid pattern is also in keeping with the room's straightforward style.

A pale sky blue on the walls of this sitting spot creates a soothing surround while staying quietly in the background at the same time, allowing the dramatic black-and-white checkerboard floor to take star status.

# • accents

Perhaps you're more comfortable adding color in small doses. Or your budget dictates taking small steps toward a new scheme. Something as small as a decorative pillow or throw can punctuate a space with attention-getting color. To find the right accent hue, look to other furnishings—even artwork—for inspiration.

And don't think that you have to match colors to a tee. It's more important that colors blend. If, for instance, you pull out a blue from a painting over the fireplace to repeat on throw pillows across the room, they'll be right at home together if they're of similar tones and intensities.

**ABOVE** In this dining room, the table and chairs, as well as the overhead light, all but disappear into the white backdrop. Even the black-painted floor seems to fade away, allowing the focus to stay squarely on the impressive work of art.

**LEFT** A simple coat of paint on the back of these bookshelves transforms the ordinary into something extraordinary. The crimson red color immediately draws the eye toward the nautical-themed collection within.

The beauty of a bright white backdrop is that colorful objects are clearly defined. Atop this mantel, two vases— one upright, one casually tipped over—are in the same color family as the nearby art, but their slightly different shades make them more noticeable.

# CHANGING A COLOR SCHEME

hanging a color scheme need not be a huge investment in time or money. The trick is to start with a neutral backdrop, one that will complement any number of colors. Instead of buying a bright red sofa, for instance, opt for one in bright white, charcoal gray, or jet black. Then, add your red hue in the form of pillows—in a mix of solids, patterns, and stripes.

If and when you tire of the red accents, simply change out the pillows to create an entirely new scheme. Because virtually any color combines well with neutrals, you're only limited by your imagination.

Incorporating color via furniture and bed linens can be expected, but don't miss smaller opportunities, either. Black-and-white patterned lampshades carry out this room's color scheme, adding visual interest that their plain white counterparts wouldn't have.

# furniture

● ● ●

CHOOSING THE RIGHT FURNITURE FOR YOUR HOME IS MUCH LIKE finding the perfect pair of shoes. You want them to be good looking, but comfort is a priority, too. Plus, it's essential that they wear well. That said, each piece of furniture in your home will have different priorities. Think about how and where it will be used. If you're shopping for a new family room sofa, for instance, comfort and durability will most likely be of prime importance. On the other hand, a sofa for a formal living room may be selected more on its style merits. But it's a good idea to go into the shopping process armed with other vital pieces of information, as well.

In addition to function, performance, and style, you'll want to consider your family's lifestyle. If it's laid-back, you may opt for chairs that family members can sprawl out on; if it's more formal, you may prefer wingback chairs. From a style point of view, does the particular piece need to match other elements in the room? What is your color scheme? As for size, be sure that your "perfect" piece will not only fit into the intended room but also through all necessary doorways.

Once you've found something that appeals to you, examine it carefully for quality; there are certain hallmarks to look for in finely crafted furniture. Open the doors and drawers of cabinets, looking not only at the joinery (where pieces of wood meet) but for ease of movement. Upholstery can be a little trickier to evaluate, but don't be timid; pick up the piece and turn it over to look for a sturdy frame and springs. These are, after all, furnishings you'll want to live with—and love—for years to come.

**Amidst rustic country-style elements—a brick floor, board-and-batten paneling, a pine wood ceiling—lively yellow chairs are a welcome change of pace, their sunny dispositions brightening the entire room.**

# sofas

● ● ● NOT ONLY IS A SOFA ONE OF THE LARGEST decorating investments you'll make, but it also represents one of the largest pieces of furniture in a room. Today's sofas are typically between 7 and 8 ft. long. When shopping for this potentially pricey item, take into consideration the sofa's depth and overall scale, as well.

A well-made sofa is typically constructed of kiln-dried hardwood such as maple or hickory, with legs that are a continuation of the frame itself—not separate pieces. Joints should be a combination of wooden dowels and metal screws and/or buttressed with corner blocks, while springs, preferably eight-way hand-tied, should be made of tempered steel. (Eight-way hand-tied springs are secured to the eight surrounding springs with heavy, knotted twine.) Last but not least, be sure that the upholstery and fill cover the inner springs well enough that you can't see or feel them.

**Classic English-arm sofas anchor this seating area, their sage green color standing out against the room's pale backdrop. At the same time, their hue is one that—like neutrals—goes with anything, allowing throw pillows to be changed out on a whim.**

**TOP** A camelback sofa like this one is often found in formal traditional settings, but its simple lines make it just as appropriate for an unpretentious country-style room.

**ABOVE** The clean and simple silhouettes of these twin sofas make them perfectly suited for a contemporary room. Their slightly curved backs lend a softness to the space that makes it more relaxing.

# sofa styles

When shopping for a sofa, you'll find there's a wealth from which to choose. Here are some of the most common styles:

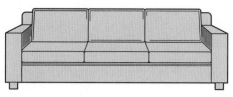

### LAWSON

A Lawson sofa has square or rolled arms that reach halfway between the seat and the top of its back, which is slightly arched or straight across.

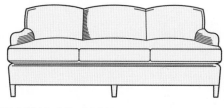

### ENGLISH OR CLUB

With a slightly rounded, set-back arm, the English or club sofa is also characterized by a tight seat and low, turned legs.

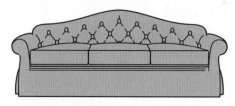

### CAMELBACK

A camelback sofa, often used in formal settings, has a serpentine line that rises from the arms to a high point in the middle of the back.

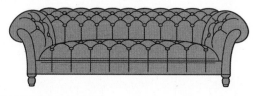

### CHESTERFIELD

Easily identified by its tufted back and rolled arms, the Chesterfield is typically upholstered in leather.

A sectional with a loose-pillow back conveys a casual feeling in this family room. The back pillows—as well as their decorative counterparts—invite rearranging for ultimate comfort.

## • sectionals

There was a time when sectional seating was reserved for modern settings. But its flexible nature is no longer limited to one certain look; sectionals can be found in every imaginable style, from the most cutting-edge contemporary to the most classic and traditional—even casual rattan and wicker.

If the designs aren't enough to choose from, there are more choices than ever in the sections themselves. In addition to armless sofas and chairs, as well as squared corners and curves, there are chaises, recliners, and sofa sleepers. It's one of the easiest ways to create a custom piece of furniture because you design it yourself, using exactly the sections you need. Best of all, sectionals can be rearranged—in the same room, a different space, or an entirely new home—providing even more flexibility in the future.

ABOVE A conventional sofa-plus-two-chairs seating group would have been an awkward fit for this bay, but the wicker sectional echoes its angular shape, making the most of every square inch of space.

BELOW This sectional and its complementary seating pieces offer the best of both worlds. They're handsome enough for any interior but, with indoor/outdoor frames and upholstery, are right at home on a porch or patio, too.

## more about...
# SOFA BEDS

**i** f you haven't taken a close look at a sofa bed lately, you may be in for a surprise. Today's versions are a vast improvement over those of the past. Not only are the mattresses much more comfortable, but the mechanisms are smoother and easier to operate, too. Sizes range from a twin, which can be tucked into a chair or ottoman, to a queen, which fits in a sofa.

Before buying a sofa bed, decide what its primary purpose will be. Is your intent to use it daily as a seating piece? If so, evaluate it by those standards first. Is it comfortable to sit on or can you feel its inner metal workings through the seat cushions? Is the construction of a high-enough quality that it will stand up to hard wear? Likewise, if it will be used as a bed on a regular basis, the comfort of the mattress will take priority, so test that out. Before buying, lie down on it as you would a standard mattress, making sure that you can't feel the bars beneath it.

# • loveseats

Loveseats can be a good option in spaces that can't accommodate oversize sofas. You can create a cozy living room group by teaming one up with a chair or two, or even a second loveseat. But loveseats aren't limited to living areas. In the foyer, a loveseat provides the perfect place to sit while changing shoes or perusing the mail. In the master bedroom, a loveseat might be placed at the foot of the bed, providing a sitting spot for your morning routine.

As with all seating pieces, be sure that your loveseat is a good fit. If you're tall, don't choose a style that is too low to the ground; when you sit, your knees will end up at your chin. Likewise, if you're short-legged, avoid pieces with extra-deep seats; otherwise, you'll find your legs sticking straight out in front of you.

An array of decorative pillows—propped against the wall—creates a comfortable back for the loveseat. Placed in the center of a room, though, this seating piece could double as a room divider, allowing guests to face either way to join a conversation.

# more about...
## PORCH SWINGS

**t**oday's casual living is by no means confined to within a home's four walls; outdoor furniture is just as functional, fashionable—and comfortable—as its indoor counterparts. A porch swing, for instance, provides a cozy conversation area for two, or for a single occupant to put his or her feet up and relax.

Hanging deck models are typically suspended from rope or chains. The swing itself can range from 4 ft. to 7 ft. in length, with teak or cedar being some of the most durable wood options. If you're looking for something more eco-friendly, you will also find recycled plastic styles in a wide variety of colors. Like any other chair, however, be sure yours is a good fit for you; seat depths can vary from 18 in. to 36 in.

**Because the seat of this porch swing is extra-deep, the owners lowered the swing closer to the slate floor, making it easier to climb into. The swing is suspended from lengths of rope that are easily adjusted.**

**With the addition of complementary back and seat cushions, a porch swing becomes even more inviting. Today, there's a wide array of indoor/outdoor fabrics that can withstand the elements.**

**Because this loveseat has no arms—and graceful curves instead of squared corners—it has a smaller profile. In this hallway, it tucks into a mere sliver of space, not impeding traffic flow in the least.**

A sage green banquette backs up to the island in this kitchen, not only providing comfortable seating but also—by its very color in the otherwise neutral room—separating working and eating areas.

# •banquettes

Banquettes—simply upholstered benches—have been called into service in kitchens for years, providing maximum seating when there's minimal space. Tucked against a wall and teamed with a table, a banquette is a comfortable place to sit and plan the week's menus, for the kids to do homework, and, of course, to eat a casual meal. But banquettes are perfectly capable of standing on their own; more and more, they're happily existing in other areas of the house—in living and dining rooms, even mudrooms. They can be streamlined, bench-only models or have completely upholstered backs. To make the most of these space-savers, it's a great idea to incorporate storage under the seat. Whether you opt for lift-up seats or drawers below, these compartments offer the best of both worlds: They keep your possessions out of sight but, at the same time, conveniently close.

With its upholstered back reaching all the way to the ceiling and covered in an eye-catching print, this banquette makes a bold statement in tandem with the pure white table and chairs.

more about...

# BENCHES

**b**enches offer some of the most versatile seating options you'll find. Prevalent in both upholstered and all-wood varieties, with or without backs, their small stature makes them a good fit for almost any space. A bench might be used in lieu of two dining chairs, or a pair of small square benches may sit at the foot of a bed. Long and narrow versions are especially good choices for front entries and back hallways, providing a place to sit and change shoes. While many benches are easily adaptable from room to room, others are site specific; a fender bench, for instance, features a U-shaped seat that wraps around the hearth of a fireplace.

A spindle-back bench in this entry—cozied up with some personality-packed throw pillows—offers a place to sit down and change shoes while coming and going.

Tucked into a corner of the great room, a low-profile upholstered bench teams up with a table that's equally small in stature, creating an out-of-the-way spot to sit and read or sip tea.

# chairs

●●● BEYOND THE PURE COMFORT THEY PROVIDE, upholstered chairs are aesthetic assets. They come in a wide variety of shapes and styles, not to mention the all-but-infinite colors and patterns. There are overstuffed club chairs, wing chairs, even those wide enough to earn the name "chair-and-a-half." Elongated chaises have a luxurious air, while diminutive tuck-aways can fit into many a nook and cranny.

No matter how big or small the chair, comfort must be part of the equation. Consider the width and depth of the seat, as well as the height of the back; for best support, it should hit the occupant at mid-back or higher. Comfort should be given especially high priority in a chair that you will use for long periods of time—like the one you sit in to watch TV. There's really only one way to determine if a certain chair is right for you: Before taking it out of the store, take it for the ultimate test drive—sit on it!

**ABOVE** The beauty of this clean-lined armchair is that it's the perfect fit in any room. Although it has a certain modern aesthetic, it's compatible with traditional and country furnishings, too.

**RIGHT** An upholstered armchair is perfectly positioned in this living room; with a table lamp on one side and a fireplace on the other, it's a comfy place to sit and read or to simply enjoy a roaring fire. At the same time, it's arranged near enough to the other seating pieces for easy conversation.

**ABOVE** A coral armchair anchors this primarily pale blue room with a solid pop of color, its graceful form silhouetted beautifully against the soft backdrop. Its curves are a welcome counterpoint, as well, to the room's numerous sharp lines and angles.

**RIGHT** This modern interpretation of a traditional wing chair offers a welcome respite, not only literally but visually, too. The pure white chair—like the white lamp and pillows—offers a "resting place" for the eye in a room full of deep, dark colors.

In lieu of a more expected pair of chairs, twin chaises flank the fireplace, providing a place for put-your-feet-up relaxation or for two to sit, face to face, and converse.

## •chaises

When the chaise originated in France—it was known as the *chaise longue*, which means "long chair"—it was strictly a bedroom piece. Its length, the equivalent of a chair and ottoman put together, provided a place to put your feet up and relax. Today, however, the chaise is just as likely to be found in the living room or even a foyer; it can be used in the

same way as a conventional sofa or loveseat, with room for two people to sit side by side.

Although the chaise has strong traditional roots, there are plenty of contemporary translations. What they all have in common is a slightly angled back that's conducive to reclining; as for arms, a chaise may have one, two, or none at all.

A modern classic, this Le Corbusier chaise takes center stage in the room. But its beauty is more than skin deep; because it's adjustable—from a nearly upright position to a full recline—it's extremely comfortable, too.

## more about...
# RECLINERS

recliners are just as comfortable as they've always been. But they're no longer instantly recognizable. Their mechanics are so well disguised that recliners are as apt to look like stationary wing chairs or Art Deco rockers. Most are still operated by a hand lever on the side, but there are also push-back models that recline when you simply lean back. Plus, there are space-saver types that require only 6 in. of space between chair and wall compared with the more standard 12 in.

No matter what kind of recliner you choose, be sure to keep some safety issues in mind. A chair shouldn't have more than 5 in. between the seat and the open leg rest; otherwise, it's a potential trap for children and pets. Likewise, be sure that the lever does not pose a pinching danger for fingers.

LEFT This antique recliner has a sculptural quality, making it just as appealing from a functional point of view as it is from an artistic one. Storage drawers beneath the seat are an added bonus.

RIGHT The high-fashion styling of these armchairs, decked out in a stylized floral print, belies the fact that they are comfortable recliners. There are no mechanisms in sight; merely pushing down on the arms allows occupants to kick back and put their feet up.

# • accent chairs

As their name implies, accent chairs can complement whatever setting they're in. Your choice may be a contemporary classic that's a work of art in its own right or a chair that has deep sentimental value. Even a colorful Adirondack chair—typically reserved for outdoor use—may be just the right accent for a family room. Adding an accent chair is one of the best ways to punctuate a room with your own personal style.

Rocking chairs also make good accents, and are perhaps more versatile in nature than any of their counterparts. They're just as likely to be found in the nursery as the family room, and are equally common in the bedroom or solarium. Wherever they are, rockers bring not only style but also a huge helping of comfort.

**ABOVE** A pair of quatrefoil-backed chairs sidle up to a small table, creating a quiet corner to sip coffee and converse. Because they're lightweight, the chairs can easily be moved to join another seating group—or even pull up to the dining table.

**RIGHT** This Shaker-style rocking chair may be an antique, but it's as appealing today as ever, thanks to a rush-woven seat with just enough give to make it ever comfortable.

There's more to this sculptural-looking chair than first meets the eye. It's not only a work of art in its own right; the body-molding form makes it far more comfortable than it might appear.

# •dining chairs

Dining tables and chairs are still widely available in matching suites, but eclectic combinations are now more the norm. Heirloom tables are apt to team up with new chairs or vice versa; a simple farmhouse table might be surrounded by chairs in a variety of styles. Whether you opt for a mixed or matched setting, keep in mind that dining chairs come with arms or without, but either must be a good fit with your table, not only from a style point of view but also in terms of height. If the table has an apron, for instance—a skirtlike extension that supports the top—armchairs need to be able to slide completely beneath or you will need to allow for extra space behind the chairs to allow passersby to walk around them.

Seating options aren't limited to conventional chairs, either. In the kitchen, a farm table might be teamed with simple wooden benches. Freestanding upholstered benches are an increasingly popular option, too, even in the most formal of dining rooms.

**ABOVE** The dining chairs around this table may all be formal in style, but by mixing things up a bit—wooden side chairs partnering with upholstered wing chairs—the room feels less staid.

**RIGHT** Modern chairs with barely-there bases seemingly float in thin air, keeping the emphasis on the sculptural red seats and, at the same time, allowing a view of the carved table base.

**FACING PAGE** The rounded backs of these dining chairs echo the form of the pedestal table so that even though they are not a matched set, they all work together as a cohesive whole.

# more about...
# SLIPCOVERS

**S**lipcovers are transformative, allowing you to change the personality of a sofa or chair in practically no time at all. If you're throwing a dinner party, don't let the guests be the only ones to get dressed up; cover everyday dining chairs with elegant slipcovers to get them into the spirit, too. Or, take a cue from Mother Nature and celebrate the changing seasons. For each, have a different set of slipcovers— a lightweight linen for spring, canvas cloth for summer, heavy cotton for fall, and warm corduroy for winter.

You can have a tight-fitting slipcover made to fit your sofa or chair like a second skin or opt for one that drapes over the piece in a looser fashion. But custom slipcovers aren't your only choice. There are plenty of ready-made slipcovers that can be "custom fitted" by adjusting an elastic edge here and a bow tie there. They're typically made of a durable material that can withstand repeated washings, too.

Cream-colored slipcovers dress up the side chairs in this dining room, their box-pleated skirts adding just a touch of flirty formality. Plus, there's a practical advantage: If spilled on, the slipcovers can be laundered.

Upholstered wing chairs may seem, at first, too formal for this down-to-earth dining area. Because they have the same sharp angles as the wood table and benches, though, they all work together beautifully.

# barstools

With today's casual lifestyles, many kitchens feature counter seating, whether to grab a quick meal, do nightly homework, or simply catch up with the cook. Because barstool heights vary, be sure to measure the height of your countertop before you go shopping. You don't want to sit so high that your knees hit the surface nor so low that you're practically hitting your chin. Check that you have plenty of knee space, too; 12 in. is recommended.

**LEFT** The wire backs of these counter stools offer welcome support. At the same time, however, they take up little visual space, a prime consideration in small spaces.

**ABOVE** For those who dine at the kitchen counter on a regular basis, upholstered stools are a good option. Not only are they more comfortable, but they also provide the opportunity to bring color into a space.

**LEFT** What were once all-wood Windsor-style counter stools have been given some feminine flair. The seats have been upholstered in natural linen, with to-the-floor matching skirts.

**LEFT** The beauty of backless stools like these is that they can slide under the counter, completely out of the way, until they are called into service. The dark twisted-leg frames of the stools stand out against the lighter wood of the island.

# ottomans

●●● OTTOMANS ARE SOME OF THE BEST multipurpose pieces you'll find; they can fit into the smallest of spaces and fulfill many a role. In addition to serving as a sitting spot—perhaps keeping a low profile in front of a fireplace—an ottoman can stand in for a conventional coffee table; one with a tightly upholstered top can steady a tray of beverages and snacks. And storage ottomans are good companions for sofa beds, providing a place to stash pillows and blankets.

For his-and-her seating at the foot of a bed, consider a pair of ottomans set side-by-side. Then put them on casters for extra flexibility, so they can easily be moved where they're needed most.

Covered in a stunning floral pattern, this ottoman is just as artistic as the prints on the wall. A form-hugging tray is a practical addition, providing a safe place to set beverages.

The pattern created by nailhead trim on the ottoman provides visual interest in this understated space. What's more, the durable burlap fabric makes sense from a functional point of view.

An oversize ottoman can serve an entire seating group. In this living room, guests seated on either the sofa or chair are within easy reach to set down a beverage or put their feet up.

## skirt styles

Upholstered seating offers an entire wardrobe of skirts from which to choose. As in fashion, however, it's important to match the "body type" with the right skirt. Pleated styles are most appropriate for tailored sofas and chairs, while those with more curves, often covered in lighter-weight cottons, lend themselves to softly gathered styles.

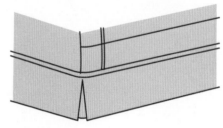

### TUXEDO

Tuxedo skirts feature a single pleat at each corner.

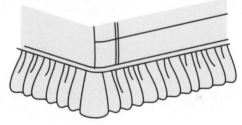

### GATHERED

Gathered skirts consist of one continuous ruffle around the bottom edge.

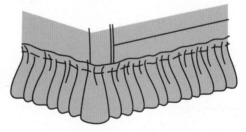

### DRESSMAKER

Dressmaker skirts also consist of one continuous ruffle but are applied on the outside and typically feature decorative welting that covers the line of stitching.

# tables

● ● ● THE VERSATILITY OF TABLES MAKES THEM particularly appealing. A kitchen table can be transformed into a homework or hobby area in a matter of minutes. A dining room table can serve up meals and, if it has lift-out leaves, accommodate anywhere from 2 to 12. The accent table that sits chairside in the living room today might be at home by your bed tomorrow. A console table in the foyer that provides a drop-off spot for mail can also back up to a sofa, holding lamps and family photographs.

There's plenty of flexibility, too, when it comes to using a variety of tables within the same space. A living room, for instance, might have a coffee table, a console table, and a couple of end tables. Your first instinct may be that they all need to have the same wood finish, but that's not necessarily so. An eclectic approach is often a better reflection of a homeowner's personality. If the tables all have classic lines and are complementary in style, you can mix and match them freely.

A see-through glass top offers a clear view of the table's artsy base, but there's a purely practical advantage, too. Glass-top tables are one of the easiest surfaces to keep clean.

The epitome of eclectic style, two distinctly different tables team up in this living room. Between two armchairs, a modern rendition provides a place for a table lamp, while—in front of it—a more traditional type offers more room for small treasures, even a beverage or two.

A leather-wrapped coffee table is central to this conversation group. It not only accommodates every seat, but also its rich brown hue visually anchors the light, cream-colored chairs.

## •dining tables

The choices you'll find in dining tables have never been more varied. In addition to the expected rectangles and ovals, there are just as many round and square shapes. The latter two can be particularly good choices if you tend to entertain in small groups; either makes conversing easier because you can see everyone without having to physically turn. Almost any dining table can be extended, too—even those that are circular; some expand via standard leaves, turning them into ovals, and others with wedges that practically double the table's diameter.

To give each diner plenty of elbow room, allow between 24 in. and 30 in. per person. If a chair falls in front of a table leg, however, allow extra room so the person in front of it can comfortably move to one side or the other.

**ABOVE** The dining table and chairs may be mixed and not matched, but they do have a common denominator. Both feature an X motif, bringing a sense of continuity and rhythm to the area.

**RIGHT** A contemporary table is placed at a right angle to the wall, the wall-hugging approach creating a more intimate ambiance than a center-of-the-room placement would have.

A simple but sturdy white-painted table takes center stage in this porch. The durable coat of paint makes for easy cleanup and can be painted over when it becomes timeworn.

# gallery

## legs and feet

Stylistically speaking, the differences in tables come down to their legs and feet. Some of the most common types are:

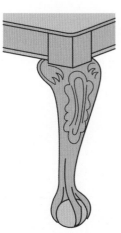

### BALL-AND-CLAW FOOT

Frequently used with a cabriole leg, the ball-and-claw foot represents a clawed dragon holding a pearl of wisdom.

### SPADE FOOT

The delicate spade foot consists of a simple square that tapers toward the bottom.

### CABRIOLE LEG

The cabriole leg resembles an animal leg with a knee, ankle, and foot, often with ornamentation at the knee such as a carved shell motif.

### MARLBOROUGH LEG

The Marlborough leg is straight and square, often ending in a block foot and featuring carved grooves its entire length.

# • console tables

A console table's distinguishing narrow depth gives it a real advantage: It can fit into many a space, even a narrow hallway. That's why it's common to find one in a front entry; the slim silhouette provides just enough space to drop off keys and mail, without impeding the flow of traffic. In a living room, a console makes sense in back of a sofa, especially if the sofa is being used to separate the room into two areas; a console table— topped with lamps and accessories—can strengthen the visual divide. And in a dining room, its slim surface provides just enough space for serving up meals. Interestingly, this type of table doesn't always have four legs. Some consoles have only front legs; the back is secured directly to the wall.

**Even homes that don't have a separate foyer can have the sense of one. In this residence, a console table teams up with a rug to create the feeling of an entry while also fulfilling one of its main functions—a place to drop keys and mail.**

**ABOVE** In a narrow hallway, even a slim console table can seem to eat up precious space. This acrylic version solves the problem beautifully, all but disappearing into the backdrop.

**LEFT** A whimsical, shell-encrusted console table may seem an unlikely companion for a rustic mirror—or a bronze sculpture, for that matter. But they're all decked out in neutral hues, and their diverse textures make for a masterful mix.

# more about...
# WORK TABLES

**S**ome of the hardest-working tables can be found in places like kitchens, laundry rooms, and craft or hobby rooms. A strategically placed table in the kitchen, for instance, might serve as an island, providing additional workspace as well as a place to sit down and eat. Likewise, a table in the laundry room is convenient for folding clothes, as is one in a hobby room for sewing or scrapbooking.

When searching for workhorse tables like these, consider "going green." Tables made of reclaimed materials often have a worn look that's inherently charming. Likewise, don't overlook antique and secondhand shops; you'll not only give an old table a new life but also, most likely, save money in the process.

Set squarely in the center of this laundry room and well lit from above, this table provides a handy place to fold clothes as well as drawer storage below.

# • coffee tables

While a coffee table is a prime display spot for collectibles, it serves a functional purpose, too, providing a place to set beverages and snacks. That's why it's important to choose one not only on its style merits but also its size. A table that's too small will look out of proportion and won't best serve those seated around it; each person should be able to reach the table easily.

As a rule of thumb, look for a model that's about two-thirds as long as your sofa. That way, everyone can access it and still easily get around each end. As for height, look for a coffee table that's approximately the same, or slightly lower, than the seats of the nearby sofas and chairs.

**TOP RIGHT** A see-through, acrylic coffee table serves its intended purpose, albeit quietly, allowing the focus to stay on superb traditional furnishings as well as the geometric area rug.

**RIGHT** A reclaimed trolley serves as a one-of-a-kind coffee table in this family room, just as spacious as it is sturdy; any nicks and scratches that might happen over time will simply add to the charm.

**ABOVE** Round coffee tables, like this beautifully grained version, partner well with L-shaped sectionals. It's easier to move around the table, plus there's no danger of hitting a sharp corner.

**LEFT** Double-duty furniture multiplies the seating capacity in this living room. Four wedge-shaped stools tuck under their companion coffee table when not in use; in an instant, though, they can be pulled up next to the fireplace or wherever they're needed.

# • accent tables

Accent tables have a chameleon-like quality; they can blend into virtually any room. It's this very trait that makes them an especially good buy for your decorating dollar. The small table that sits next to the sofa today may work just as well bedside in the future—adaptability at its best. Nesting tables, for instance, fall into this category. Typically found in sets of three, their gradually stepped-down sizes fit beneath one another; then, they can be pulled out as needed. Drum tables are popular options, too, as are butler's tables with lift-off tray tops that are convenient for entertaining. In short, the variety of accent table styles is as vast as their placement possibilities.

This sleek white accent table tucks between two just-as-contemporary armchairs, anchoring an out-of-the-way sitting spot perfect for quiet conversation or a cup of tea.

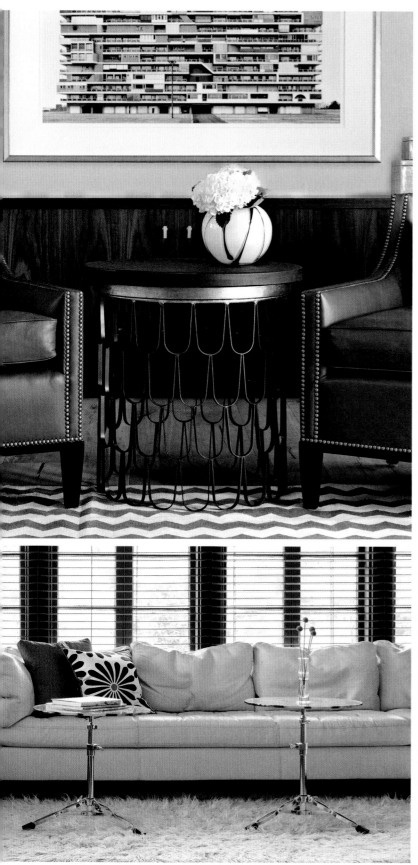

## more about...
# BEDSIDE TABLES

**b**edside tables need not be limited to the conventional two-drawer types. Any table can work; just be sure that the height is no more than 2 in. higher or lower than the bed so you can easily reach bedside essentials such as a lamp, book, or alarm clock. Think in terms of double-duty pieces, too. A writing desk, for instance, can accommodate your bedside needs and stand ready when you need to catch up on some correspondence. Likewise, a small dresser can serve its original purpose and that of a bedside table.

This nightstand goes the extra mile by providing shelf storage for books and magazines as well as a drawer to keep small items corralled. There's even a pull-out shelf for those times when the tabletop surface gets crowded.

**TOP LEFT** The graceful styling of this accent table belies its strength. Rows of sturdy metal loops form the base of the table, supporting a nearly indestructible zinc top.

**LEFT** In front of the sofa, a pair of small accent tables stands in for a more conventional coffee table. Not only do their chrome-and-glass silhouettes take up less physical and visual space in this alcove, but they're easier to walk around, too.

# desks

● ● ●   WHETHER YOU ARE A TELECOMMUTER OR simply need a convenient place to pay bills, a desk of some kind is a necessity. At one end of the spectrum are slim writing tables that can be incorporated into almost any room. Their small size doesn't mean they aren't hardworking, though. In fact, writing desks are some of today's best multipurpose pieces; in the dining room, for instance, one can double as a buffet.

At the other extreme, oversize partners' desks can be an instant focal point in a family room or library. What's best for you comes down to a decision of how much table surface and storage you need. For some, that may be no more than enough space to set a laptop, while others may require more room to spread out and multiple file drawers, too.

**RIGHT** A substantial desk in this home office is strategically arranged, taking full advantage of the room's natural light during the day. At night, or whenever it's needed, a floor lamp stands ready to shine more light on any subject.

**BELOW** A wrap-around writing desk keeps every necessity within easy reach. Backed up to a bay window, this cream-colored conversation piece is showcased beautifully against the darker curtains.

This delicate writing table slips into a corner, accommodating a lamp and a few accessories as well as space to pay bills, catch up on correspondence, or set a laptop.

b uilt-in desks, long commonplace in the kitchen, have now moved beyond. Today, you're likely to find them anywhere—in the family room, bedroom, even a well-outfitted craft room. Because built-in desks are made to your exact dimensions, they bring with them the advantage of custom compartments. Whether it's extra-large papers or odd-size objects such as docking stations for handheld electronics, storage can be shaped to suit your own needs.

Conversely, in this day and age, when nothing more than a laptop and a wireless connection are needed to conduct business, you may only require a sliver of space. A small-scale desk will fit into many a nook or cranny, even under a window where it can take advantage of the natural light. Leave room beneath it for a lightweight bench or simply keep a lightweight chair nearby that can be pulled up as needed.

This built-in desk utilizes minimal space, providing a work surface for a laptop as well as artistically arranged drawer and shelf storage. The coral color peeking out from underneath only furthers the artistic impression.

# • double-duty desks

Secretaries, rolltops, and drop-lid desks come with all kinds of compartments and cubbyholes, making them good choices for those who take organization to the nth degree. Plus, with a quick flip of the lid, you can quickly conceal any clutter. In today's smaller spaces, these kinds of desks are also attractive for another reason. They typically feature drawers below the work surface and—in the case of secretaries—shelves above it, too. In fact, a secretary is often made up of a drop-lid desk with a hutch on top; it comes in two parts to make moving it easier. While the design roots of all of these are steeped in tradition, their efficient use of space makes them perfectly suited for today's interiors.

**The traditional secretary desk gets a modern-day twist in this living room. Its sleek, angular form tucks neatly between two windows, providing plenty of drawer storage and the customary drop-lid desk, too.**

**TOP LEFT** A small desk doubles as a nightstand in this master retreat, accommodating every bedside necessity. When deskwork is on the agenda, a lightweight chair can be called into service from another corner of the room.

**TOP RIGHT** A handy desk surface slides out from the middle of this breakfront, delivering desktop space or merely more room for accessories. When it's not needed, the surface simply slides back and takes on the appearance of just another drawer.

**LEFT** In a do-it-all family room, this tabletop slides out from beneath the TV, ready to be used for homework, a light meal, or even for putting puzzles together.

# beds

● ● ● THE BED IS THE UNCONTESTED FOCAL point of any sleeping spot. Its commanding presence immediately sets the tone—and the style—of a room. From curtained canopies to commanding four-posters, you'll find beds in every imaginable style.

No bed is complete, though, without the right mattress. Nothing less than a full size (also referred to as double or standard) is recommended for a single adult; believe it or not, a twin bed is only as wide as a crib. Most people prefer queen- or king-size beds, and there are options for tall people, too. A California king, for instance, is 4 in. longer than a conventional king-size mattress, although you'll give up 4 in. in width. Before buying any mattress, however, be sure to take it for a "test drive." Lie down in your usual sleeping position, then move around a little and even sit on the edge. Don't be swayed by "firm" or "soft" labels, either; what's most important is that the mattress feels right to you.

**ABOVE** A fanciful four-poster is the undeniable star of this bedroom, its dark wood turnings piercing the space in grand fashion. The rest of the room's furnishings are intentionally simple, keeping the emphasis on the impressive piece.

**RIGHT** A four-poster is commonly known as a Cannonball bed, a reference to its origins in Colonial times. This one spans the space between two windows, including them and the nightstands below as part of the focal-point sleeping spot.

**FACING PAGE** A handsome rattan bed infuses this bedroom with the feeling of a tropical retreat, its intricately detailed form shown off beautifully by the contrasting pristine white linens.

# • metal beds

The quintessential brass bed has been cherished for years, its gleaming frame invariably the focal point of a room. Though many brass beds feature the metal in its natural state, which develops a soft patina over time, there are additional options. Some beds are given a clear lacquer finish that can simply be wiped clean; it takes less upkeep than natural brass, but there's a trade-off in terms of authenticity. Meanwhile, other finishes can give brass a completely different look; a nickel-plated coating, for instance, gives traditional brass an updated appearance.

Beds made of iron, whether they're hand-wrought or machine-made, are another perennial favorite. Their finishes are nearly as varied as the styles themselves; in addition to natural black, you'll find bronze, pewter, and even painted pieces.

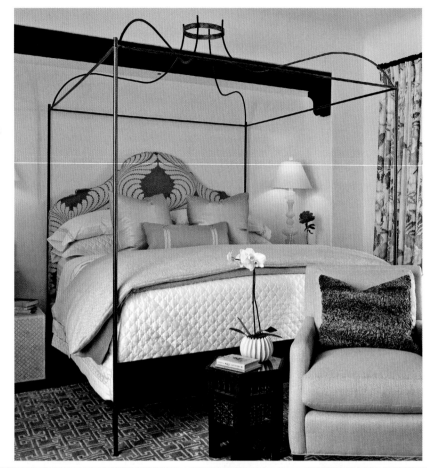

**TOP RIGHT** The graceful curves of this metal tester bed, topped with a crown, bring an element of softness to a room filled with straight lines and sharp angles.

**RIGHT** Antique brass beds, like the one in this girl's room, require a bit more care—and elbow grease—than those with lacquered finishes, but the tradeoff is much more authentic charm.

# INNOVATIVE HEADBOARDS

Personal style is at its best when you incorporate one-of-a-kind decorating ideas. And headboards are a good place to start. Their inherent flat, vertical shape lends them to multiple translations. Do you have a preference for cottage-style spaces? Cover a piece of plywood—the same width as the bed—with brightly patterned oilcloth; the material will not only add a bright splash of color but also its surface is easy to wipe clean. Or, take a similar approach with vinyl-coated wall coverings, available in virtually any style.

Unique headboards can be fashioned from almost anything, even moldings applied directly to the wall.

A matched pair of colorful, artfully carved doors serves as a headboard in this otherwise neutral bedroom, creating an instant focal point. Because they reach nearly to the ceiling, they draw the eye upward, making the room seem taller in the process.

An antique folding screen still serves its original decorative purpose while standing in as a headboard. The upper lattice portion even makes it easy to hang over-the-bed works of art.

Even if you don't have a curtained canopy bed, you can create the look of one. In this bedroom, ceiling-suspended rods support gauzy curtains that cozy up the sleeping spot.

## • upholstered beds

Today's vast assortment of bed linens puts no limit on the color and pattern you can bring to a room. But upholstered beds take the concept one step further, allowing the sleeping spot itself to make a dazzling impact. Part of the appeal is that an upholstered bed can be just as subdued or spectacular as you like. You can choose from headboard-only options, even wood-framed styles that make it easy to change out the material as the mood strikes. Or, you might opt for a fully upholstered piece. Likewise, the fabric that you select can make a world of difference. A bed wrapped in a dramatic black, for instance, will make a completely different statement than one enveloped in a bright color.

# more about...
# PLATFORM BEDS

t he clean-lined nature of platform beds gives them a contemporary air. Consisting of nothing more than a flat surface that supports a mattress, this type of sleeping spot eliminates the need for a box spring. Be sure, however, to use a mattress intended for this kind of bed.

Platform beds, often made of metal or wood, can be found with or without a headboard. This style of bed has its physical advantages, too. Because it's lower to the floor (due to the absence of the box spring), a platform bed is easy to get in and out of.

A sturdy wooden platform beneath this bed sets the tone for this room's down-to-earth neutral scheme; it's just as minimalistic as the rest of the decor.

A black leather-upholstered bed makes a dramatic impact in this cream-colored room. Without the button tufting, the bed may have appeared too plain but, as is, has just the right amount of subtle pattern.

# ●twin beds and daybeds

Twin beds are a smart choice for a child's room, providing sleeping space for the child and a guest. But they aren't just for kids; in a guest room, twin beds offer key flexibility. They can be positioned individually, with a nightstand between to serve them both. When need be, they can be pushed together, creating the equivalent of a king-size sleeping spot.

Daybeds, meanwhile, have the same kind of adaptability. A daybed can serve as a combination sofa/sleeper in the living room or home office. One with an open back can even be used to bridge two separate seating groups, allowing the occupant to join either conversation.

**ABOVE** A daybed in this child's room echoes the modern color scheme established by the area rug. It's the perfect place for story time or to curl up and take a nap.

**TOP** To fit this pair of twin beds neatly under the windows, they've simply been turned on end. The footboard is now at the head of the bed, while the original headboard makes for an impressive foot.

**ABOVE** A set of upholstered twin beds in this guest room is as unpretentious as the rest of the room. They're simply dressed in covers with the look of moving blankets—as hardworking as they are hardwearing.

# • bunk beds

A good choice for rooms short on space, bunk beds make the best use of every vertical inch. Typically, this type of bed—which can be freestanding or built-in—consists of two twin-size mattresses stacked atop one another; in some cases, you'll find a full-size bed on the bottom and a smaller twin on top. And you need not have two kids sharing a room for bunk beds to make sense; they can be ever ready to accommodate overnight guests.

For safety's sake, guardrails are highly recommended on the top bunk, especially when small children are climbing up there. It's also important that the top bed not be too close to the ceiling; otherwise, the occupant will hit his or her head every time he or she sits up. Finally, to make bed-making easier, choose linens that you can simply pull up and tuck in.

**ABOVE** Bunk beds with a nautical theme make perfect sense in this seaside room. One of the most efficient ways to sleep several people, bunks are fun for kids but sophisticated enough for grown-ups, too.

**TOP** Instead of the typical one-on-top-of-the-other arrangement, this set of bunk beds takes a fresh approach. The lower bunk is positioned at a right angle to the upper one, creating a cozy play space between the two.

**ABOVE** Built-in bunks in this boys' room make the most of every square inch, carving out enough space to sleep four. Each compartment is fitted with a slim wall light, too, making it easy to read in bed.

# room arrangements

• • •

SMART FURNITURE PLACEMENT ALLOWS YOU TO FUNCTION WITHIN A ROOM in the most comfortable way. You can carry on a conversation in the living room without passersby walking between you and whomever you're talking to. You can pull out a dining room chair without hitting the sideboard behind it.

Some of the best room arrangements are those viewed from a fresh perspective. Look at your space with no preconceived notions, wiping previous room arrangements from your memory. Ask a friend or family member for an opinion, or even call in a design pro. You might be surprised how simple the solution may be; a piece pulled from another room, for instance, can get a new lease on life in a different spot.

Many rooms will give you clues to furniture selection and placement. If, for instance, you have a living room with a fireplace, a nearby conversation area is a natural. Or, if you have a long and narrow space, consider creating multiple groupings. At one end of the room, the main conversation area might focus on a fireplace while an informal dining area occupies the other end. To further drive home the point of separate spaces, underscore each with an area rug that defines its boundaries.

**Breaking tradition with the conventional sofa-plus-two-chairs arrangement, this conversation group comprises four cozy armchairs in front of the fireplace. All four have easy access to the ottoman, too, handy for holding a tray of drinks or offering put-your-feet-up comfort.**

When considering room arrangements, don't be locked in by room labels, either. Just because one space is designated as the living room and a slightly smaller one for dining doesn't mean they have to be used that way. If, for instance, you host extended-family meals on a regular basis, switching the rooms around may be a more comfortable fit.

# floor plan pointers

●●● VISUALIZING THE PERFECT FLOOR PLAN IN A bare space can be overwhelming. That's why it's important to do your homework. Using a piece of ¼-in. grid paper, draw a to-scale outline of your room, including every door and window. Then, from a separate sheet, cut to-scale templates that represent the furnishings you have as well as the ones you need. (You can also purchase magnetized floor plan kits or use one of the many room arrangement programs available on the Internet.)

Spend some time playing with various room arrangements until you come up with one that works for you and your family. Then, make a list of the pieces you'll need to purchase—noting their dimensions—and keep it with you during the shopping process. This relatively small investment in time will keep you from making costly miscues later.

**RIGHT** By painting the backs of the bookcases the room's predominant blue hue, the built-ins take on a more custom appearance. The deep color also seems to bring forward the architectural elements, making them more of an integral part of the room.

**BELOW** An L-shaped sofa and pair of upholstered chairs provide plenty of seating in this living area while not taking up too much visual space. The greige sofa blends into similarly colored walls, while the chairs—because they're armless—have slim silhouettes.

Tucked into a half-wall between the living and dining areas, a banquette teams up with two rattan chairs, creating a place to eat that's both comfy and cozy. The chairs are lightweight enough to be moved to the living room when needed.

# WHY THIS ROOM WORKS

*i*n an open floor plan, like this stepped-up living/ dining area, colors are your best bet to keep things cohesive. A neutral-and-blue scheme flows throughout the area, the cool hues creating a calming effect. Equally relaxing are the simple, straightforward furnishings; an overabundance of pieces can make a room feel chaotic. Here instead, an L-shaped sectional anchors the main conversation area, its neutral upholstery blending quietly into the background of the same color. Completing the seating group is a pair of armless blue chairs, their streamlined silhouettes taking up minimal physical—and visual—space in the relatively small quarters. Meanwhile, a square ottoman does double duty; because the top of the piece is tightly upholstered, it can serve as a coffee table, too.

Up a couple of steps, a dining spot utilizes the rooms' separating half-wall in the best way imaginable: Banquette seating backs up to the wall itself, teaming with a simple table and pair of armless chairs to create a cozy eating area.

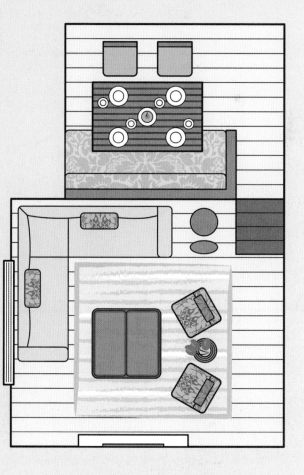

# the living room

●●● WHETHER IT CONSISTS OF TWO SOFAS OR several club chairs encircling a cocktail table, a conversation grouping is at the core of every living room. When formulating your own floor plan, keep in mind that people are most comfortable sitting directly across from one another or at right angles to each other. So even if your sofa can physically accommodate four, plan on it seating no more than two or three at a time.

When planning sufficient seating for guests, don't feel that you need to fill the room with sofas and chairs to accommodate everyone. Benches, ottomans, and even nearby dining room chairs can be called into service as necessary. Small upholstered cubes are a good choice, too; when not in use, they can tuck away under a table.

**A symmetrical arrangement, in which the furniture in one half of the room mirrors the other, invariably creates a soothing, easy-on-the-eye ambiance. The pair of low benches at one end is a good choice, too; taller seating pieces would have stopped the eye, making the conversation area seem smaller.**

**ABOVE** Apple green upholstered pieces ground this seating group that can easily accommodate four. Rounding out the arrangement are a pair of armchairs with hot pink seats and two zebra-patterned benches that quickly double the capacity. They're easy to move around the room or into another one entirely.

**LEFT** The white sectional sofa and matching chair in this room would have faded away against all-white walls. Here, though—with a contrasting pale blue backdrop and gray-blue rug beneath—their solid structure defines the room in the same way that walls would.

**ABOVE** In spite of this sectional's generous size—it can easily accommodate six—it comes off as cozy. By splitting the seating piece in half, each side invites people to curl up in comfort in front of the flat-screen TV.

**FACING PAGE** This family room is arranged so each seat has a clear view of the television, as well as the fireplace. Twin leather-framed sofas define the size of the seating group, complemented by two blue suede chairs that—because they're deeper in color—visually balance the larger sofas.

## elements of design
# TEXTURE

@ visually appealing mix of textures is essential to any room. Nowhere, though, is it more important than in a room primarily decked out in neutral hues. Consider for a moment a room with seating pieces covered in linen and curtains made of the same material, combined with a wooden coffee table and hardwood floor in similar colors and matte finishes. Light coming into the room will hit all of the surfaces in a similar way, resulting in a sameness overall. Take that same room and leave the linen seating intact, but replace the curtains with polished cotton, change out the coffee table for one made of metal and glass, and add a sisal rug to the hardwood floor. The various surfaces will reflect in different ways, creating more visually interesting highlights and lowlights throughout the room.

**In this living room, polished wood end tables contrast with the woven raffia of the coffee table, while the smooth linen upholstery of the twin sofas contrasts with the plush velvet of the green armchairs. The crowning touch? A pair of ceramic lamps and a mirror over the fireplace reflect light off of their shiny surfaces.**

# the dining room

●●● IT TAKES MORE THAN ANY OLD TABLE AND chairs to create a comfortable dining room; the best ones are those furnished comfortably enough to make you want to linger well after dessert. If you're wondering what table shape will best suit your room, look no further than the shape of the room itself. Rectangular and oval-shaped tables are best for long and narrow rooms, while round or square tables fit neatly into square-shaped spaces. Whatever the shape of your table, though, allow 2½ ft. to 3 ft. behind each chair so occupants can get in and out easily.

When choosing dining chairs, it's largely a matter of personal preference; armless styles fit under a table more easily, but armchairs can be more comfortable because they provide a place to rest your elbows.

**In a formal dining room with a fireplace, arrange the table and chairs in front of it—just as a seating group would be in a living room. Upholstered chairs like these are a good choice for a formal setting. Not only are they dressier than their wood counterparts, but they're more comfortable, too, for long and leisurely meals.**

**ABOVE** Many an oversize space is divided into living and dining areas. In this open floor plan, the dining area is defined as much by the table and chairs as it is by the chandelier over them.

**BELOW** The patterned upholstery of these dining chairs beautifully picks up the table's soft shade of yellow, making them perfect partners. Although the dining space is formal, the vibrant colors give the room a more casual atmosphere.

# RHYTHM AND HARMONY

Some basic design principles are essential to any well-designed room, rhythm being one of the most important. Visual rhythm flows throughout a room, gracefully leading the eye from one design element to the next. You can create rhythm with a particular pattern or motif. Likewise, with textures, you can keep the eye moving around the room with shiny glass here, a soft rug there, and a rough-hewn table somewhere in between.

In a successful room scheme, there also needs to be a sense of harmony. Fabrics, for instance, should be a good fit for their frames. Denim is fine for the family room sofa but ill suited for a French bergère chair. Finishes should be more refined in formal spaces and more relaxed in casual quarters. Color is critical, too. By running a common thread of color throughout, various elements of a room will come together to form a harmonious whole.

There's a distinct sense of rhythm in this dining room, thanks to a circle theme running throughout. Circles are not only found on chair backs but also in the mirror, chandelier, and even the artwork.

# the great room

●●● THE TYPICAL GREAT ROOM DOES IT ALL, providing a combination living/dining area, often opening onto a kitchen. Floating furniture arrangements work best in these rooms, with large pieces such as sofas dividing them into more intimate areas. Strategic room arrangements can direct traffic, allowing people to pass through a room without interrupting a gathering deep in conversation.

Because the great room, by nature, is a generously sized space, it's particularly important to plot this room arrangement on paper first. Start by placing major pieces of furniture, add tables and rugs, and finally position each individual table and floor lamp.

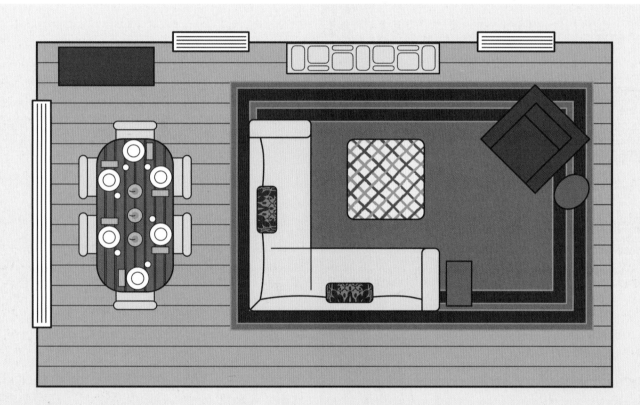

## WHY THIS ROOM WORKS

using an L-shaped sectional is one of the easiest ways to divide and conquer a large space. A high-backed version like this one, nearly the same height as a half-wall, immediately creates the feeling of two rooms. In front of the fireplace, a conversation group comprises pieces in square and rectangular forms,

creating a cohesive sense of rhythm. From the sectional and armchair to the ottoman and end tables—even an area rug and the fireplace itself—there's a distinct sense of connection simply in their forms.

In contrast, the adjacent dining area—its sense of space created by the back of the sectional as well as a

chandelier centered overhead—relies on common circular and oval shapes to unify it. The oval tabletop and chair backs plus round shapes in the chandelier and candlesticks contribute to the sense of two separate spaces.

**ABOVE** A fireplace provides a natural focal point in a room. In this great room, the main conversation group gathers in front of the fireplace, defined further by the Oriental rug beneath.

**BELOW** An oval-shaped table anchors the dining area, its white-painted chairs standing out prominently against the dark piece. Because it has a tall back, the nearby sofa further helps create the feeling of a separate eating spot.

# SCALE AND PROPORTION

In design terms, scale refers to the relationships among furnishings within a room. An oversize wing chair, for instance, may not be the perfect partner for a diminutive wooden chair. And it's more than physical size that comes into play; visual weight is equally important. Most homeowners, for instance, put some kind of table or chest on each side of the bed. If you prefer not to use matching pieces—and as an increasing number of rooms fall under the eclectic umbrella, that's the case more often than not—be sure that your choices are compatible in size and scale.

Similarly, a good sense of proportion is essential to any well-designed room. A table, for example, should be in proportion to the sofa it is next to, and the lamp, in turn, should be in proportion to the table it's on. There are some guidelines to help you know if the relationship is right; an end table, for instance, should be no more than 2 in. higher or lower than the arm of the sofa it's next to. Beyond basic guidelines, though, it's up to your eye to decide if a room's proportions are in line.

Not only are the furnishings in this living room all of a similar scale, but their visual weights are well balanced, too. Because the sofa, for instance—the largest piece in the room—is light in color, it quietly blends into the background. Had it been upholstered in a dark hue, it would have overpowered the other seating pieces.

# OPEN FLOOR PLANS

Open floor plans come with their own challenges. There are few walls against which to place pieces of furniture and even those that are in place are often half-walls. Instead, you're more apt to find structural columns that have to be blended into the room arrangement. But the good news is this: You can turn those columns into architectural assets with a little careful planning.

An intrusive column in the kitchen, for instance, can be the cornerstone of a custom built-in. Space permitting, you might build out the column, creating wrap-around, floor-to-ceiling storage. Or use the column to anchor a central island, making it an integral part of the design.

Likewise, assume you have two columns 12 ft. apart near the middle of a long and narrow space. You can position a sofa between the columns facing one end of the room, where it immediately becomes the foundation of a conversation area. In back of the sofa, place a server that can house essential tabletop items for the dining area. At once, those potentially problematic columns will establish room parameters, blending quietly into the background at the same time.

**In a long and narrow space, furnishings echo that same shape. A pair of sofas face off in front of the fireplace, creating a cozy conversation area. Meanwhile, a rectangular dining table at the other end of the room runs parallel to a kitchen island of nearly the same size.**

**TOP AND ABOVE** Creating distinct living and dining areas isn't only a challenge indoors; generously sized decks can present the same kind of hurdle. The solution can be as simple, however, as orienting the seating group in one direction with the dining area at a right angle to it.

**RIGHT** A load-bearing column could have been intrusive in this kitchen. Instead, it's made part of the master plan by incorporating it into an island. The entire element is copper clad like the rest of the room's cabinetry.

# the bedroom

●●● MORE THAN MERE SLEEPING SPOTS, TODAY'S bedrooms are all-hours retreats, with designated areas for reading, watching television, even catching up on correspondence. That doesn't mean that the bed will be secondary; its sheer size invariably makes it the focal point of any room. Still, other activity areas should be placed far enough from it so while one person is enjoying a TV program, for instance, the other can sleep undisturbed.

Because it's the undisputed focal point, the bed should always be the first consideration in your room arrangement. Be sure to allow sufficient space to make it each morning; 2 ft. on each side is recommended. When positioning a dresser or nightstand, provide at least 36 in. of space in front of the piece of furniture. Otherwise, you'll find it a tight fit every time you try to open a drawer.

**Floor coverings can divide a room of any size or shape into distinct zones. In this bedroom, the sleeping area—including the bed as well as bedside tables and a pair of ottomans—is completely underscored by an area rug, while a reading spot sits off in a corner atop the white-painted floor.**

**ABOVE** In this master retreat, an alcove naturally creates the sense of distinct sleeping and living areas. Further emphasis, though, is provided by cream-colored area rugs that anchor the two spaces.

**LEFT** This fireside sitting area instantly has the feeling of a separate space, merely by arranging the chairs with their backs to the bed—and allowing for easy traffic flow between them.

# window treatments

●●●

THE WINDOW TREATMENTS IN A ROOM ARE OFTEN THE UNSUNG HEROES. More than mere decorative elements, they control light, provide privacy, and even conserve energy.

For example, if you have a bedroom with an east-facing window, an opaque window treatment such as lined curtains or wooden blinds will keep the sun from waking you before the alarm. And in the bathroom, where privacy is a priority, the right shade—when lowered—can fill the bill but, when raised, stack to a fraction of its length, allowing you to take in a beautiful view.

Window treatments can reflect a fashion sense just like a wardrobe. A traditionalist may opt for something opulent such as sheer curtains teamed up with floor-length draperies and topped with elegant swags and jabots, lengths of draped-and-looped fabric with "tails" hanging on each end. On the other hand, a minimalist might feel more at home with tailored Roman shades. There are plenty of eco-friendly options, as well, ranging from organic cotton curtains to roller shades made of natural materials.

**Curtains in this master bedroom not only dress the window. The treatment also extends behind the headboard, the soft folds creating another layer of textural interest— important in a room with subdued hues.**

What's more, the right covering can visually alter the dimensions of a window. A conventional double-hung style, for instance, will seem taller with curtains that reach from the top of the frame all the way to the floor. To give the same window even more importance, extend the width of the treatment by using a wider-than-necessary rod; when the curtains are completely open, they'll fully reveal the panes of glass but leave the impression that the window is wider than its actual dimensions.

# draperies

● ● ● DRAPERIES ARE OFTEN DISTINGUISHED FROM curtains by their level of elegance; draperies are thought to be formal, while curtains are assumed to have a more casual air. In fact, however, the differences are more technical than anything else. By definition, draperies are suspended from hooks attached to a traverse rod that can be highly decorative or all but invisible. They're opened and closed with a pull cord and are typically lined and sometimes even interlined— an additional lining, between the primary one and the decorative fabric, that can make the treatment less see-through or simply add weight so that it drapes better.

Often paired with top treatments such as valances and cornices or swags and jabots, draperies can be elaborately trimmed. A beaded fringe might run up the panels' inside edges, for instance, or a more subtle braid might border both sides and the bottom.

**This formal drapery treatment is in keeping with the bedroom's overall traditional style. The side panels pull back far enough to allow easy access through the French doors to the outdoor balcony, while a matching valance conceals the necessary hardware.**

## more about...
# PICKING THE RIGHT FABRIC

**W**hen choosing a fabric for a window treatment, it's important to match the material to the style. If you're considering gathered curtains, for instance, the material should easily drape into soft folds; light- to medium-weight cottons are good choices as is sumptuous silk. On the other hand, flat curtain panels as well as many shades call for fabrics with a little more body; linen and cotton canvas, for example, can stand up to the challenge.

At the same time, take a close look at the fabric's pattern. Solid colors and medium-size prints work just about anywhere, but fabrics with large pattern repeats (the side-to-side measurement of the motif) are better for window treatments that are equally large in scale. To appreciate an intricate pattern to its fullest, make sure that it doesn't get lost in too many folds of fabrics.

**TOP LEFT** The sheer size of this window wall gives it focal-point importance, taken to yet another level with the eye-catching graphic motif of the drapery. It carries out the coffee-and-cream color scheme established by the room's furniture and contrasts beautifully with the woven shades.

**LEFT** When a window treatment is this tall, drapery—with a traverse rod and pull cord—is the easiest and best way to open and close the panels. If, however, privacy isn't a concern and there's no need to close them, stationary side panels work perfectly well.

# •curtains

Curtains, unlike draperies, are typically unlined; plus, they open and close manually. Still, they don't give up a thing in style. Hung from stationary rods, they can be suspended from shirred rod pockets, tab tops, even oversize grommets. They can be coupled with valances and cornices, too—casual translations of draperies' more formal renditions.

A curtain's length depends, to a large degree, on its intended purpose and place. Small windows, for instance, may be dressed with curtains that reach only as far as the sill or the bottom of the window's apron (frame). Tall windows, on the other hand, often call for floor-length curtains, or—for a more dramatic impact—panels that puddle a few inches on the floor.

Red-and-white curtains in this living room not only add color and pattern to an otherwise neutral scheme but they also make the room seem taller with their floor-to-ceiling panels, which draw the eye upward.

## CUSTOMIZE READY-MADES

If you have your eye on a stunning window treatment, but it's too much for your budget to bear, translate the look by customizing simple ready-made panels. Perhaps you've found a pair of sumptuous silk curtains trimmed with tassel trim, also made of silk. To bring the cost down, opt instead for ready-made curtains in a silky polished cotton, then add tassel trim made of cotton, too. Or, simply trim panels with tape trim, perhaps in a straight line down the inside edges or culminating in a Greek key motif.

You can take the concept a step further by customizing tiebacks. For those same silk-like curtains, embellish the tiebacks with a complementary braid. Or, take your creativity to yet another level and look for everyday items that will play up a room's personality. In a little girl's room, for instance, use colorful stretch headbands or inexpensive bead necklaces to hold the curtains in place.

Damask-patterned curtains add visual interest to this monochromatic scheme, their motif made more prominent against solid-color walls and a tailored Roman shade, both in the same creamy hue.

A strip of red fabric edges these custom bedroom curtains, echoing the accent color established by the nearby lamp. The same effect could be achieved by applying tape trim along the edges of ready-made curtains.

While beds are often positioned against a solid wall, a large window can serve as a backdrop, too. This white-upholstered bed is framed by the window's blue-and-white curtains, giving the sleeping spot more importance—and dimension.

# more about...
## SHEER CURTAINS

**S**heers have long passed the point of being all white. Today you'll find a wide variety of colors in gauzy cottons, filmy voiles, and even see-through lace. Just as many have patterns, too, ranging from geometric plaids and stripes to those with softer floral motifs.

Due to the delicate nature of sheers, it's important to keep the styling simple; most come with conventional rod-pocket or tab tops. Or, make your own perfectly flat panels—hemmed on all four sides. You can hang them from a slender rod with metal clips or add oversize grommets along the top edge and suspend the sheers with ribbon.

Patterned sheers in this master bath are in keeping with the room's spa-like appearance. They're backed by solid privacy curtains, which also make the sheers' pattern stand out more prominently.

Sheer curtains gently filter the light streaming into this sunroom. Oversize grommets along the top edges, threaded on a white metal rod that blends into the backdrop, make it easy to pull the curtains open and closed.

French doors call for lightweight curtains that can be moved out of the way with ease at a moment's notice. Sheers fill the bill here, their cream color blending beautifully with the room's neutral scheme.

Windows span two entire walls of this bedroom, which could have made privacy an issue. Instead, cream-colored curtains run the entire length, teamed up with matching Roman shades to create a cocoon-like effect.

# gallery

## curtain calls

While curtains are the perfect companions for windows, they're by no means limited to that single use. Simple curtain panels can be utilized in a number of ways. A curtain, for instance, might be used in place of a door; whether used to conceal storage or to define separate rooms, curtains are considerably less expensive than their architectural counterparts—not to mention that they're easier to install. What's more, curtains provide more options in terms of color and pattern, providing an opportunity to put your personal stamp on a space.

There's no hard-and-fast rule that curtains are limited to the indoors. Ticking-stripe panels flank the columns of this back deck, creating the feeling of an enclosure without blocking the view or the fresh air.

Sheers draping the doorway to this dining room add patterned interest to the otherwise solid colors throughout. By simply pulling them shut, the eating area instantly becomes a much more intimate place.

In this girl's bedroom, bubblegum pink curtains disguise open-shelf storage on either side of the window, keeping things neat and tidy—and easily accessible—while adding a splash of color at the same time.

# • valances and cornices

The crowning touch on many a window treatment, valances and cornices can be purely decorative or serve a specific function. Valances, typically made of pleated or gathered fabric, provide a soft look, while cornices, characteristically made of plywood that's painted or wrapped with fabric, as the name implies, create a more architectural effect. Both, however, are just tall enough to discreetly disguise nondecorative hardware, including rods, hooks and rings, and pulley systems.

Both types of top treatments can be used alone, too, adding just the right touch of decorative element or a splash of color. At a kitchen window, for example, a short valance can complement the room's color scheme and, at the same time, stay high and dry above a sink full of suds.

**ABOVE** A turquoise-upholstered cornice echoes the accent color of its companion Roman shade, then takes teamwork a step further by repeating the green of the soft treatment in covered buttons and welt trim.

**RIGHT** A simple white valance dresses the bay window in this kitchen, lending softness to the angular architectural element. It's short enough, too, not to be affected by splashes from the sink below.

To allow maximum light in this butler's pantry, the window was intentionally left unadorned—with the exception of a scalloped cornice at the top that adds a subtle but striking decorative element.

# DECORATIVE HARDWARE

decorative rods may support window treatments of all kinds, but they by no means settle for supporting roles. They're co-stars more often than not, carefully chosen to complement their fabric counterparts. Metal finishes continue to be popular, including conventional brass and wrought iron but also encompassing burnished bronze, brushed nickel, aged pewter, and even copper. You'll find real metals as well as resin-cast look-alikes, which provide the heavy metal look without the weight. For contemporary interiors, wire rods are another option—lightweight curtains are simply attached to a length of wire with decorative clips.

Wooden poles are still a perfectly viable option. Beyond the wide variety of painted and stained finishes—even those that look like bamboo—there are also unpainted alternatives that you can finish yourself. Keep in mind that whatever material you choose, finials can make a distinct decorative difference. Some rods come with finials attached, while others give you the option of choosing your own, including everything from scrolls and spears to leaves and flowers, even colored glass.

Patterned curtains are suspended from this wooden rod by matching rings, the dark color of the hardware complementing the curtain fabric. The element of surprise is the white flower-like finial; its shape and contrasting color immediately draw the eye to the window treatment.

window treatments 113

# blinds and shades

● ● ● THE DISTINCTION BETWEEN BLINDS AND shades is nearly as subtle as that between draperies and curtains. Blinds are typically hard-edged, made of stable materials such as wood, vinyl, or aluminum. In contrast, shades take a softer approach; they're usually made of some type of fabric—or at least materials, such as natural bamboo, that fall into soft folds like fabric does.

Both blinds and shades have practicality at their core, controlling light and privacy. That said, however, they come in a wide variety of fashionable designs. Slatted blinds, for instance, run the style gamut from ½-in. vinyl mini-blinds to 2-in.-wide metal Venetian blinds. Wooden blinds are well suited to traditional décor, while vertical blinds are more contemporary in nature. Their slats can be encased in sheer fabric, too, allowing light to gently filter into a room. Likewise, shades offer a wealth of choices. Roman shades, balloon shades, roller shades—even shades woven from natural materials—can be just as casual or upscale as the rest of your decor.

Three tailored Roman shades dress three identical windows in this family room, adding delicate color and pattern to the muted scheme, whether lowered a little or a lot. They lend continuity to the backdrop, as well, carrying out the same motif found in the French doors' curtains.

**LEFT** In this dining room, blue-and-white Roman shades afford the only pattern in the space, making them an instant focal point. Given even more emphasis with their blue tape trim, they lead the eye to the windows and to the view beyond.

**ABOVE** Pleated shades come in a rainbow of colors, allowing you to match virtually any hue. Here, though, they blend into the windows' white trim, making them all but disappear when pulled up completely.

**LEFT** The angular shape of the bay window is accentuated with crisp Roman shades. Their sage green hue is an attention-getting contrast to the wall color, providing enough visual weight to balance the large expanse of glass.

# •balloon and roman shades

A balloon shade can be easily identified: As it's raised, this type of window treatment gathers into voluminous folds. When lowered completely, the gathers are barely visible. The right kind of fabric is imperative, though. A lightweight cotton or silk—or anything that easily falls into soft folds—is best suited for the style. Fabrics such as heavy linen or glazed chintz, on the other hand, won't "balloon" but, instead, result in a stiff look. Plus, heavy materials make a balloon shade more difficult to lower and raise.

Roman shades are more tailored in their appearance. In the down position, they hang completely flat but, as they're raised, create horizontal pleats that are typically 6 in. wide. In fact, when pulled up all the way, Roman shades look more like a crisp valance than a shade at all. Fabric choice is important for this treatment, too; best are those that will hold a pleat, like linen, or even natural materials such as bamboo.

**TOP RIGHT** A striped Roman shade runs the length of this triple window, its strong vertical pattern directing the eye toward the bathroom's uncontested focal point—a freestanding tub. Although the shade can be fully extended for privacy, there's no need as companion shutters fill the bill.

**RIGHT** Balloon shades—with their characteristic rounded bottoms and "tails" on each side—team up with more tailored Roman shades in this girl's bedroom, the tandem treatment carrying out the lively pink-and-green scheme.

Roman shades can be mounted outside the window frame or inside, as in this casual eating area. Here, that inside-mount option allows you to fully appreciate the architecture of the bay window as well as the blue-and-white toile treatments.

# MEASURING WINDOWS

**b**efore purchasing any window treatment, it's vital that you take some careful measurements. Use a steel measuring tape (a cloth one can stretch, and being off even a fraction of an inch can make a difference) and always round up to the nearest ⅛ in. For inside-mount treatments, only length and width measurements are needed. For the length, measure from the bottom of the window frame to the top of the sill (A). For the width, measure from side to side on the inside of the frame (B). Be sure, however, to measure at the top, middle, and bottom; because your measurements may vary slightly, use the smallest number.

For outside-mount treatments, you'll also need to measure the area to the left (C) and to the right (D) of the window that will be covered. For shades, this may be only to the outside edge of the window frame; for draperies and curtains, it will depend on how wide you want the finished treatment to be. You'll also need to measure the distance from the top of the window opening to wherever your hardware will be located (E). This will typically be on the window frame itself for shades and well above the frame for curtains and draperies; it might be as far up as the ceiling, depending on the look you want. Finally, measure from the top of the sill down to the point at which you want your window treatment to stop (F).

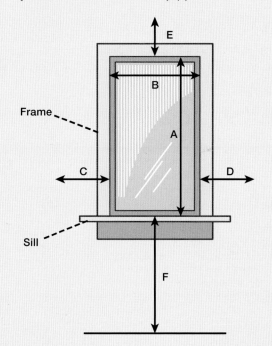

# • woven shades

Made of natural materials, woven shades are one of today's most eco-friendly options. Small horizontal strips of bamboo, cane, grass, or various other reeds are simply sewn together to fashion roll-up or Roman-style shades. Due to the way it's constructed, this type of window treatment allows light to softly filter through. But if your preference is a completely dark room, a blackout lining should be added.

Woven shades are often used in tandem with other window treatments; they can, for example, tuck neatly under a valance or cornice. And their inherent neutral hues complement any color. They can also stand alone, in which case it's best to choose a style with a self-valance that hides the hardware at the top.

**ABOVE** To keep this dining room open and airy, the entire bank of windows is treated in simple woven shades, their open weave allowing light to gently filter into the space.

**LEFT** Multiple windows can be given individual woven shades or share a single one. In this dining room, the latter option lends continuity; although the room's windows aren't identical, their treatments are.

**FACING PAGE** Red-and-cream curtains pop color and pattern into this family room, while companion woven shades take care of the heavy lifting, controlling both light and privacy yet not overpowering the decorative treatments.

# more about...
## PLEATED SHADES

@s their name implies, pleated shades are simply that: shades made of durable fabric or paper that fold into uniform accordion pleats. The beauty of these window treatments is that they suit windows of any size or shape, even arches and skylights. Plus, they are available in a virtual rainbow of colors, patterns, and textures. They pair well with curtains and draperies, too, although they can just as well stand on their own.

Fully extended, pleated shades provide privacy and light control but, when open, the pleats stack compactly—to an inch or two—so you can take in the view. Most operate from top to bottom, although some can be raised from the bottom. Pleated shades are typically controlled with cords but, if there are small children in the house, consider cordless options for safety reasons.

**While gentle swags add an air of elegance to this master bath, the companion pleated shades provide the necessary privacy. When not needed, however, they pull up completely, hidden beneath the swag treatment.**

# • wooden blinds and shutters

Today's wooden blinds offer much more than the expected brown hues and rectangular shapes. Although warm wood tones are perennially popular, you're just as likely to find these blinds in a wide variety of colorful paints and stains, accented with plain or patterned cotton tapes. They can fit windows both arched or angled, even French doors, and vertical wood blinds can be installed on sliding glass doors. The beauty of wooden blinds goes beyond their aesthetic value. The moveable slats—which can range in width from 1 in. to 2½ in.—can be opened to allow maximum light into a room or closed to provide privacy and keep in the heat on a chilly day.

Shutters instantly add architectural interest. Most common are traditional shutters and their Plantation-style counterparts. Traditional types are characterized by 1¼-in. louvers and are particularly well suited to small windows; their narrow louvers block the sun's strongest rays but, at the same time, limit your view. Plantation shutters, with louvers typically 2½ in. and 3½ in. wide, are a better fit for large expanses of glass; with their wider louvers, they provide more drama, as well as a better view of the outdoors.

**Simple plank shutters are apropos in this mountain home, their appearance as rustic as their surroundings. When privacy is needed, they fold out to span the entire width of the window.**

**TOP LEFT** The rectangular shape of shutters makes them just as suitable for doorways as windows. Tall shutters in the passageway between this living and dining room afford the possibility of more privacy for both spaces.

**TOP RIGHT** While true wood blinds may not be moisture resistant—and not the best fit for a bathroom—there are plenty of look-alikes that are. There's nary a clue that these blinds aren't the real thing, right down to the traditional tape trim.

**LEFT** Shutters in a bathroom offer the ultimate in privacy and light control. They can be opened completely, allowing sunshine to flood the space, or tightly closed, letting in not so much as a ray of light.

# wall coverings

● ● ●

THE WALL COVERINGS YOU CHOOSE DESERVE CAREFUL CONSIDERATION, if for no other reason than they add up to more square footage than any other surface in a room. That translates to quite a commitment not only in terms of color and pattern but also cost.

The variety of wall coverings available today is nothing short of vast. Paint options offer far more than a single color brushed onto the walls; bold color combinations are increasingly prevalent. Wallpaper has recently seen a resurgence in popularity, not only because of its fashion-forward patterns but also because it offers some innovative surfaces. In addition to more conventional types, you'll find grasscloth and even glass-beaded papers. There are even three-dimensional wall coverings that can be painted your color of choice. And considering all the types of tile that are wall-appropriate—from sparkling ceramic to rich wood—it's clear there's a creative solution for every room.

When choosing a wall covering, there are some basic guidelines to keep in mind. If a room's furnishings are bold, you'll want to make the walls more subdued and vice versa. Additionally, maintenance will come into play; easy-to-clean wall coverings are necessary if there are children or pets in the house. Most important, though, let your imagination go.

**Proof that sometimes less is more, this stylized floral wallpaper makes a greater impact teamed with crisp white wainscoting than it would have on its own. The wainscoting not only provides a welcome contrast but also visual relief from the busy pattern.**

# paint

● ● ● ONE OF PAINT'S BEST ATTRIBUTES IS THAT IT'S affordable. Plus, it offers instant gratification. In a matter of hours, you can completely transform the look of a room and, if or when you tire of a certain shade, you can paint right over it again. There are literally thousands of colors from which to choose, but if you don't find the precise one you're looking for, go the custom route. Your paint dealer can match any hue—a fabric, a flower, even a child's favorite crayon.

The paint industry has made great eco-friendly strides. Most major manufacturers now offer environmentally safe options with low volatile organic compounds (VOCs). While this type of paint is available in a more limited palette, it's void of that "new paint smell" and, because VOCs contain toxic substances, it is a healthier option.

**Turquoise-painted walls, a perfect match for the bed linens, wrap this room in a blanket of soothing serenity. Cool hues— blues, greens, and purples—are always a good choice in sleeping spots due to their calming nature.**

**ABOVE** A simple coat of paint can give timeworn paneling a new lease on life. This playroom takes that concept to another level, however, with a whimsical mural on one wall.

The angled wall could have been viewed as problematic, but—with a stylized nature-inspired mural—it's turned into a focal point instead.

## PICKING THE RIGHT PAINT

**b**ecause not all paints are created equal, it's important to choose the right one for your particular job. Generally, latex is the paint of choice for interiors; this water-based paint is not only durable but also easy to clean. The most common types of latex are:

**Flat:** Because this type of paint is the least scrubbable, it's best reserved for low-trafficked areas such as formal living and dining areas and master bedrooms.

**Eggshell:** More washable than flat latex, eggshell finishes are characterized by a subtle sheen.

**Satin:** Paints with a satin finish are versatile; slightly glossier than eggshell paints, they're durable enough for almost any room.

**Semigloss:** The relatively high sheen of semigloss paints is well suited to kids' rooms, which get a lot of wear and tear, as well as moisture-prone spaces such as bathrooms.

**High-gloss:** This type of paint is the most durable, making it a good choice for woodwork and trim. It can be highly dramatic, too; a dining room with high-gloss walls will literally sparkle with candlelight.

## more about...
# PLAY SPACES

f you don't have the luxury of designating an entire room to a play space, consider creating one within the four walls of a child's room; it can provide everything his or her imagination needs. It can be as simple as carving out a corner, defined by a colorful rug on which kids can stretch out and color or read. Likewise, space beneath a lofted bed can create the sense of a separate play area. But if you have a room with generous dimensions, consider building a specific structure. Your child will have a place to "get away" and play with friends—real or imaginary—right under the safety of your own roof.

**TOP RIGHT A** previously under-utilized corner now accommodates a "two-story" play space. The stairs to the second level are safely to one side, while steel supports assure it's a solid structure.

**RIGHT A** bump-out about the same size as a standard double closet transforms into a playhouse in this girl's room. An entrance as well as peepholes were created by simply cutting circles out of the drywall.

When using an intense color like this red-orange, it's important to balance the hue with more subdued neutrals. White cabinetry and a slate floor fill that role here, keeping the wall color from seeming overpowering.

t's erasable, washable, and extremely durable. And if you think chalkboard paint is only available in conventional black or green colors, think again; it comes in a wide array of hues. Application is easy, too: Simply apply it to your chosen surface, then let it cure for three days before using it.

Consider a chalkboard in the kitchen for grocery lists, phone messages, or the family's chore list. Paint a chalkboard wall in a child's room to spur creativity. Or designate a chalkboard space in a home office, then add a piece of decorative molding at the bottom to hold the necessary chalk.

A sliding barn-style door between a family room and guest bedroom does more than provide the necessary privacy. Given a coat of chalkboard paint, it also serves as a convenient place for messages and even a game board.

# wallpaper

● ● ● WALLPAPER IS CURRENTLY ENJOYING AN unprecedented wave of popularity. Styles range from traditional florals to retro pop-art prints. Colors run the gamut from the most subdued hues to surprising combinations. And, given the green movement, there are a wide variety of natural textures, too. In short, there's a style to suit everyone's taste.

But the attraction goes beyond pure aesthetics; technological advances have made wallpaper even more attractive. In addition to conventional rolls, there are varieties that don't require adhesive at all. Simply wet the paper and put it in place; when you're ready for a new look, the wall covering peels right off without damaging the walls. It's a particularly good option for kids that grow up quickly—or renters looking for just as much style as those who own their homes.

**The cream-colored background of the wall covering is a welcome counterpoint for this study's abundance of dark wood trim. Meanwhile, the simple pattern complements—and doesn't compete with—the architecture.**

Grasscloth-covered walls in this guest room stay quietly in the background, allowing the twin beds to take center stage. At the same time, their texture keeps them visually interesting, not at all bland or boring.

# CREATE A CUSTOM WALL COVERING

There's a wall covering to suit every type of decor, but one of your own creation can take personal style to an entirely new level. If writing is your passion, for instance, completely cover one wall of your home office with pages torn from an old dictionary or thesaurus (add a clear topcoat to keep the corners from curling). Or, if you're a pianist, take a similar approach with favorite pieces of sheet music. A map-themed wall covering could also be created with oversize maps, new or antique—like those once used in schoolrooms.

Flea markets and tag sales can be great sources of inexpensive possibilities. More than likely, the biggest investment you'll make is the time you spend dreaming up the perfect wall concept.

Because the young occupant of this bedroom has an adventurous spirit, a giant map of the world creates the perfect focal-point wall.

With a large doorway on one side leading to the living room and an open staircase on the other, this foyer may not have four walls, but it's clearly defined by strategically placed wallpaper.

**ABOVE** A graphic wallpaper was the inspiration for this room's entire color scheme. Seating pieces, for example, feature the wall covering's soft shades but are in solid tones that don't compete with the pattern.

**RIGHT** Taking a cue from the traditional marble-topped cabinetry, the wallpaper in this bathroom is just as classic in tone. In a space that, with all of its faucets and fittings can seem cold, the gold pattern adds a layer of warmth.

A close look at this modern wallpaper reveals its striped pattern, offset by wooden shelves that bring equilibrium to its vertical lines in a dark neutral hue that balances the profusion of color.

## WALL DECALS

In nurseries and kids' rooms, where young occupants are growing and changing fast enough to make your head spin, wall decals can be a smart choice. In lieu of time-consuming painted motifs and murals, wall decals are quick and simple to apply and affordable, too. What's more, they peel off just as easily; you can reposition them to your heart's content.

Wall decals aren't limited to kids' motifs, however. Graphic dots and stripes, animal prints, even dry-erase maps and message boards are among the many options. With wall decals, you can literally change the look of a room in minutes!

The wall decals in this nursery are just as contemporary as the rest of the room's furnishings. A pair of stylized trees overlook the crib, their bright pops of color just the thing to attract a baby's attention.

A diminutive powder room presents the opportunity to use a more whimsical, out-of-the-ordinary wall covering, one that might be too strong in large doses or in a larger space.

# fabric

●●● WALLS COVERED IN FABRIC ARE SOMETIMES considered a fashion statement more than anything else. But, in truth, they're also hardworking; fabric-covered walls are equally adept at disguising surface imperfections. Your fabric of choice can be glued, nailed, or stapled directly onto the wall; put a layer of batting beneath it to add a layer of insulation and create a sound barrier. Or, you can pleat it, shirr it, or drape it to add more of a three-dimensional look.

Fabric can even be used to create walls where there are none. You might, for instance, take a cue from the Victorian era and curtain off a doorway; when privacy is a priority—or you simply want to hide a room from view—simply pull the curtain across the door. Likewise, suspend a floor-length curtain from a ceiling to divide an oversize space into more intimate areas.

Lengths of extra-wide fabric tape were used to create this one-of-a-kind wall covering. After applying a burlap-like material directly to the wall, the fabric tape was simply woven on top of it.

**ABOVE** Complementary floral prints dress the wall panels of this bedroom, in much the same way as a patchwork quilt. A common color—pink—ties the varied patterns together, repeated in soft furnishings throughout.

**FACING PAGE** A black-and-white toile fabric wraps this room's walls and ceiling, even appearing on window shades and the bedskirt. The result is a cozy, cocoon-like effect, perfectly fitting for a bedroom.

# wood

●●● THERE WAS A TIME WHEN WOOD PANELING was all similar in style, with the look of 4-in.-wide boards running vertically from floor to ceiling or, on a smaller scale, 1-in.-wide beadboard. But times, not to mention technology and personal tastes, have changed. Today's offerings still include these perennially popular styles but also encompass architecturally intricate traditional designs, complete with all manner of moldings and trim, as well as cutting-edge contemporary looks. The latter includes pressed plywood forms with raised circle motifs, offered in the same types of wood as any other paneling—birch, cherry, and walnut—as well as natural cork.

Additionally, reclaimed and recycled wood panels are a good fit for both traditional and country-style rooms. But there's no need to feel compelled to wrap your walls with wood from top to bottom; a wainscoted look can be just as attractive. Some manufacturers make it easy, too, by offering precut panels that are the standard 32 in. high.

**Wood has an inherent warmth, making it a good choice for cozy living quarters. This library is outfitted in floor-to-ceiling pine paneling, complemented by a cool green-painted ceiling to balance the temperature of the room.**

Wood paneling that has seen better days can be painted to give it a fresh appearance. In this living room, sage green walls have a calming effect while adding just a touch of color to the otherwise neutral scheme.

Typically associated with traditional style, wood paneling gets a contemporary twist in this bathroom. Square panels are outlined with metal strips, resulting in a geometric wall pattern.

## more about...
# MOLDINGS

I n an architecturally lackluster room, decorative moldings can save the day. A chair rail, for instance, can add dimension to a traditional interior. This type of molding originally had a practical purpose; it literally kept chair backs from bumping against the wall. Today, however, it typically serves a decorative function. Install one approximately 3 ft. to 4 ft. from the floor, or about one-third of the way up the wall.

At ceiling level, crown or cove and at floor level, baseboard moldings can be equally impressive. Purchased in preformed pieces—either wood or polyurethane (which looks like plaster)—they can be painted to color-coordinate with your room. There's no need to limit yourself to a single molding type, either; use multiples to create a one-of-a-kind effect.

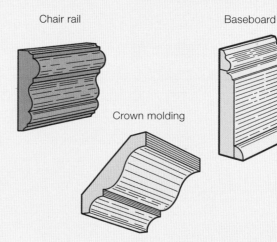

Chair rail

Baseboard

Crown molding

**ABOVE** The wainscoting in this bath is painted the same cream color as the upper walls—and the cabinetry, for that matter—creating a pale backdrop that allows the antique faucet and basin to stand out prominently.

**LEFT** Sage green–painted paneling in this masculine retreat features a slight striation, giving the wall treatment an aged appearance although it's brand-new. This shade of green is a good choice, too, because—like neutrals—it works well with practically any other hue.

# more about...
## RECLAIMED WOOD

**b** y their very definition, reclaimed materials are those that have been used before and then reused without reprocessing. They're often adapted in some way—perhaps cut to a different size and shape, or refinished—but basically retain their original character. Lengths of wood originally used to construct bleachers, for instance, might find a new life as wall paneling.

Much of today's reclaimed wood comes from old barns and industrial buildings, although sources also include everything from boxcars to wine barrels. Whatever the origin, wall treatments fabricated from reclaimed wood have an inherent charm. Not only are they an eco-friendly option, but there's also a certain vintage appeal that brings instant warmth to a room.

**ABOVE** Short pieces of reclaimed wood stack from floor to ceiling, creating a one-of-a-kind accent wall. The varied colors of the individual pieces make it even more eye-catching.

**LEFT** Simple 2x4s arranged horizontally wrap the walls of this bedroom. Interspersing painted lengths of wood among those naturally finished results in a subtle striped effect.

# tile

● ● ● CERAMIC TILE IS A NATURAL IN THE KITCHEN and bath, where it's easy to clean and can stand up to high moisture. But its hardworking nature isn't its only asset. A wide variety of colors and patterns also makes it versatile from a design standpoint. Ceramic tiles offer some of today's most stylish solutions, whether they're highly decorative, creating a complex mural, or showcasing solid colors in a creative way. In fact, solid-color tiles can be configured in almost innumerable ways, from simple checkerboard patterns to intricate, interlocking motifs.

When putting in ceramic tile, don't assume that white grout is your only option. Though essential to any tile installation, grout can play a decorative role, too. It can be tinted to subtly blend into the overall design or—in a contrasting shade—inspire an entire color scheme.

**ABOVE** Taking a design cue from the room's round sink, the tile that graces this bathroom wall features interlocking circles, softening a space typically filled with hard surfaces.

**RIGHT** Strategically placed tiles—large white squares interspersed with blue tile strips—create a striped effect in this bathroom, complemented by mosaic tiles in a slightly lighter shade of blue lining the enclosed shower.

Three distinctively different tiles team up to give this bathroom its singular style. Charcoal-colored pavers run across the floor and on up the wall, punctuated by decorative tiles that define the wash-up spot. The nearby shower, meanwhile, is a complete contrast, lined with cream-colored marble tiles.

## more about...
# TILE TYPES

t he types of tiles appropriate for wall applications go far beyond ceramic and glass. Porcelain is harder and more durable than either one and has a distinctively sophisticated look. Lacquer tiles, with nearly 20 coats applied by hand, have a highly polished finish that's compatible with contemporary schemes. Likewise, metal has a modern look; these tiles can be found in a wide variety of finishes, from brass and bronze to aluminum and stainless steel. Concrete, typically in more subdued hues, comes in a surprising number of textures and shapes as do wall tiles made of leather.

As an alternative to more conventional paneling, wood is now available in tile form, too. Dense woods like mesquite work well because they warp very little. From a green point of view, cork is attractive; it's sustainably harvested from the cork oak tree.

# gallery

## backsplashes

There are certain parameters when it comes to a backsplash. Certainly, it needs to be able to resist food stains and water. But, because a backsplash runs behind not only countertops but often the cooktop, too, it has to be able to stand up to heat. Once those standards are met, however, the sky is the limit in terms of style—a backsplash can set the tone for a room's overall color scheme or offer a striking contrast. And while ceramic tile is the most often-used material, you'll find a number of other materials that meet the requirements.

Wallpaper, like this whimsical example, is a perfectly viable option as a backsplash as long as it's heat and water resistant. There are more vinyl-coated wall coverings on the market today than ever before.

Simple gray and white mosaic tiles create an elaborate damask pattern behind this cooktop. By limiting the design to one small area, it makes a greater impact in the room.

**ABOVE** A backsplash made of marble tiles establishes an air of elegance and is the perfect companion for a marble countertop—often a baker's top choice for kneading or rolling out dough.

**LEFT** The brick backsplash contains the same warm tones as the red-painted cabinetry around it. Warm colors are a welcome complement to the cool metal in kitchen surfaces, from utensils to cooktops.

# • glass tile

Glass tile has recently enjoyed a renaissance; it's more popular today than ever before in its centuries-old history. The difference lies in its increased versatility—you're apt to find it not only on walls but also ceilings, floors, and countertops—and its palette, which is practically limitless.

Shimmering glass mosaics can add sparkle to any space, reflecting light and infusing more life into a room. Plus, this type of wall covering has practical advantages. Like ceramic, glass tile is water resistant, making it a good choice in kitchens and baths that are moisture prone. Then there's the eco-friendly advantage. Because glass tiles can be made of 100 percent postindustrial or postconsumer recycled content, the soda bottle you sip from today could well end up on your walls tomorrow.

**TOP RIGHT** Pale green glass tiles in this bathroom establish a refreshing feeling, their color that of cool, clear water. Further enhancing the ambiance are uncomplicated elements, such as the simple white basin.

**RIGHT** Set against a backdrop of cream-colored ceramic tiles, red and orange glass mosaics seem to shine more brightly, thanks not only to the contrast in color but the contrast in finish, too.

# more about...
## GLASS BLOCK

**g**lass block is typically used in rooms where privacy is required but a certain amount of light is needed. You'll find it, for instance, in bathrooms, used in lieu of conventional windows. More and more, however, glass block is also playing a purely decorative role. A row of glass block over a standard double-hung window can give the look of a light-filtering transom or, backlit along the bottom edge of a tub, it can provide a dramatic glow.

When shopping for glass block, you'll find a wide range of textures, from those that are completely see-through to those that have a frosted finish. There's even an alternative to heavyweight glass; if your application requires something more lightweight, consider acrylic look-alikes.

**ABOVE** Six strategically placed glass tiles provide the necessary privacy in this master bath, while gently filtering light at the same time. Each is treated as a window in its own right, with the ability to open and allow fresh air in.

**LEFT** Glass blocks form the walls of this walk-in shower, gently filtering light from the window beyond. What's more, this type of surface is easy to keep clean.

# the fifth wall

●●● THE FIFTH WALL IN A ROOM—THE CEILING—deserves just as much attention as the four walls that rise to meet it or the floor that it mirrors in size. Given its generous dimensions, there's any number of ways to treat a ceiling. Paint it a shade darker or lighter than the walls themselves; a darker color will seemingly advance, making the ceiling appear lower for a more intimate feel, while a lighter hue will recede, making the room feel taller in the process.

You might also opt to use the same paper that covers the walls, creating a cozy, cocoon-like feeling. Or go for a look that's a complete contrast: Add a Victorian-style tin ceiling—or an embossed wall covering that's painted silver to look like one.

**ABOVE** Covered in the same wood paneling used on the walls, the ceiling of this kitchen completes the clean white backdrop, complementing—yet, just as important, not competing with—the room's other architectural strengths, like the shuttered cabinetry doors and transom windows.

**RIGHT** The fresh approach to this bedroom includes a coffered ceiling that doesn't sport the typical square or rectangular panels between beams. Instead, it takes a more irregular tack, creating a pattern that's a work of art in its own right.

The panels in the coffered ceiling are painted a rich chocolate brown, echoing the hue used over the fireplace and giving more importance to the white-painted beams in the process.

# floor
# coverings

• • •

CHOOSING THE RIGHT FLOOR COVERING COMES DOWN TO A BALANCING ACT. The expanse of space provides the opportunity to make a dramatic impact, but at the same time, there are practical considerations. Like every decorating decision you make, this selection process should begin by answering some basic questions. First, how much do you have to spend? There are stylish options at every price point, so be frank with yourself about your budget. For your kitchen, for example, you'll find vinyl that replicates the look of marble, giving you the function of the former and the look of the latter—all without spending a fortune.

Next, consider the room that the floor is in: Who will be using it and how? Is it a living room used mostly by grown-ups? Is it a family room where small children will undoubtedly give any floor its fair share of wear and tear? Give some thought, as well, to comfort; a forgiving cork floor in the kitchen, for instance, is easier to stand on for long periods of time than hard ceramic tile. Finally, look ahead to care and maintenance. A gleaming hardwood floor, for example, is a handsome flooring option and easy to keep clean. But, if there are dogs or cats in the house—with nails that will unquestionably scratch it—be prepared to refinish the floor from time to time.

**An area rug with a modern motif establishes the color scheme in this living room. Because the rest of the furnishings are in softer, solid hues, the floor covering gets star status.**

# carpet

● ● ● THE POPULARITY OF CARPET IS EASY TO understand: With nearly unlimited color choices, it can provide a starting point for a room's scheme or complement furnishings already in place. Plus, it's comfortable underfoot, reducing noise and conserving energy at the same time by providing a layer of insulation. What's more, there are lots of eco-friendly carpet options.

Carpet types include synthetics, such as nylon and polyester, as well as natural fibers, like silk and wool. Whatever your preference, be sure that you purchase the best your budget allows, especially in highly trafficked areas. One test of quality is to check the number of yarns per square inch; the higher the number, the better the quality. You can also perform a simple "grin" test. Fold a carpet sample in half, back to back, to see how much of the backing is exposed. The less you see, the denser—and more long lasting—your carpet will be.

## more about...
## CARPET TILES

ⓘ n the past few years, carpet tiles have made tremendous strides. They're still just as easy to install—if not more so—but the variety in color and pattern far exceeds the limited palette of the past. With today's carpet tiles, you can create a wall-to-wall look, a bordered rug, even a runner for the front hallway. Not only does this type of flooring bring with it endless opportunities for one-of-a-kind style, but there's also an economical advantage. If one of the tiles gets stained or damaged, you can simply replace it instead of the entire floor covering.

In step with current technology, many of today's designs are made from recycled or renewable resources. Some manufacturers have even gone the extra mile and will recycle the tiles when you're ready to retire them.

Chocolate brown carpet may not, at first, seem a likely choice for a nursery. Here, though, the rich neutral is the perfect counterpoint, making the room's hot pink accents stand out prominently.

**Simply turning these carpet tiles at right angles to one another creates a more eye-catching pattern. In fact, there's no limit to the number of patterns that can be created with this type of floor covering.**

**ABOVE** Carpet is often the floor covering of choice in bedrooms, for both aesthetic and practical reasons. Not only does it come in practically limitless colors, but it's soft and warm underfoot, as well.

**BELOW** A navy, star-studded carpet anchors this bedroom, providing a welcome dose of pattern in the otherwise white surround. It serves as the springboard, too, for the room's red, white, and blue scheme.

a working knowledge of carpet terminology will help you make better shopping decisions. Each type has different characteristics and, as a result, wears differently. Basically, carpet can be categorized into one of three basic types:

**Cut pile:** The yarns in a cut-pile carpet are sheared at the top, allowing them to stand up straight. Some cut-pile carpets fall into the category of plush, which is often used in bedrooms and living rooms; the longer the yarn, the more luxurious it feels. Frieze carpets also have a cut pile, but the yarns are tightly twisted and, thus, more hardwearing, making this type of floor covering a better choice for highly trafficked rooms.

**Loop pile:** This type of carpet, in which the loops are left intact, can be of the level-loop variety (with loops all the same height) or multilevel loop, with slight variations throughout. One of the most popular kinds of loop-pile carpet is berber, a good choice for great rooms because of its durability.

**Cut-and-loop pile:** Combining the two basic carpet types, a cut-and-loop-pile carpet features both cut and uncut yarns, giving it a subtle, sculpted pattern. It's a good option for rooms that get heavy use because footprints are disguised by the pattern.

A green-and-white-striped area rug defines the sitting spot. Cotton, flat-weave rugs like this one come in a multitude of colors and patterns and are inexpensive, too.

## • rugs and runners

Area rugs are appreciated most for the color and pattern they can bring to a room. But they're more hardworking than they're often given credit for. An area rug can define a specific conversation area, plus there's the comfort factor. The right area rug can soften, physically and visually, hard floor coverings such as wood and tile.

There's a vast assortment of types from which to choose, but some of the most popular area rugs are:

**Aubusson:** This tightly woven tapestry-style rug is flat-woven, making it durable. A handmade Aubusson, especially one made of all wool, can be expensive.

**Braided:** Most often round or oval in shape, this type of rug—with strong Colonial roots—consists of one continuous braid.

**Oriental:** Authentic Oriental rugs are hand-knotted of wool or silk, making them expensive, too. A less expensive alternative is a machine-made rug that replicates authentic Oriental-style motifs.

**Kilim:** These wool rugs are flat-woven and often reversible, making them last twice as long.

**t**he size of the area rug you choose depends solely on where it will be used. But to take the guesswork out of the equation, there are some basic guidelines. Start by putting your floor plan on paper, then experiment with standard rug sizes; they typically run the gamut from 2x3 ft. to 9x12 ft. The right rug should either be large enough so that all of your seating pieces fit comfortably on top of it or large enough for the front legs of each to fit. (Don't mix the two concepts; the sofa, for instance, shouldn't be completely on the rug while an accompanying chair can only fit its two front feet.) Similarly, in the dining room, an area rug beneath your table and chairs should be big enough to accommodate all of the pieces comfortably—with chairs pulled out as they are when being used.

**TOP LEFT** A dramatic black-and-white area rug—a work of art in its own right—is the undisputed focal point of this screened porch. But the beauty of the floor covering is more than skin deep; its indoor/outdoor construction allows it to stand up to the elements.

**LEFT** While the rest of the room, in cool greens and crisp whites, establishes a soothing spa-like ambiance, a hooked rug in the center of the space lends warmth—both visually and literally.

Oriental rugs need not be reserved for traditional rooms. This one is right at home in a more relaxed setting, anchored by a casually slipcovered sofa.

# STAIRWAYS

a carpet runner going up a set of stairs visually leads the eye from one level of a home to another. But there are practical advantages, too. In addition to minimizing the wear and tear on stairs, these soft, sound-insulating floor coverings also keep noise to a minimum.

Runners present a variety of design opportunities. They can quietly blend into the stairs, or provide a stark contrast. Either way, a runner should create a sense of continuity, complementing furnishings on the first floor and those at the top of the stairs, too. You might also opt to add decorative stair rods. They should measure at least 1½ in. longer than the width of your runner and can be capped on both ends with finials.

The carpet runner used on the stairs matches the striped pattern of those in the hallways. Brass rods keep the stair runner securely in place, while a white border defines the edges, echoing the crisp white walls and trim.

This colorfully striped carpet could have easily been turned at a right angle at the landing. Instead, the pattern was placed on the diagonal at that point, leading the eye around the corner and upping the visual appeal.

**ABOVE** An area rug in sophisticated shades of charcoal gray delivers a welcome contrast in this otherwise monochromatic room, allowing each piece of furniture to stand out instead of fading away.

**LEFT** Braided rugs are quintessential additions to any country-style room—their subtle colors are appropriately unpretentious and their tight construction fittingly hardworking and long wearing.

# • natural fibers

Today's casual lifestyles call for floor coverings that are just as laid back. And that's where natural fibers come into play. Whether it's sisal or seagrass, coir or jute, these types of floor coverings are durable enough to be used almost anywhere in the house. Because they're relatively inexpensive, they won't take a big bite out of your decorating budget, either.

In its natural state, this type of flooring comes in soft shades of cream, brown, and green. But it can be dyed to take on other colors and patterns. You'll find rich colors, such as red and gold, as well as graphic patterns, like stripes and checkerboards. Border trims—from simple cotton twills to tapestry-like edgings—can be added as well for an extra decorative touch.

**Although casual in feeling, natural-fiber rugs are right at home in more formal settings, too. In this living room, a neutral-hued sisal rug softens the hard-wood floor while staying quietly in the background, allowing the furnishings to take center stage.**

**No longer limited to basic beige, natural-fiber rugs can be found in a variety of colors, textures, and patterns, proven by this smart-looking, black-striped example.**

In a formal dining room such as this, a natural-fiber rug could have come off as too casual. Simply by edging it in the same spring green used as an accent throughout, its style status is elevated.

# RUG LINERS AND PADS

t o keep an area rug from slipping, no matter how large or small, you'll need to put the right liner beneath it. There are two different types, however, so be sure to select the right one. The first is used when putting a rug on top of a hard surface, such as wood or tile; the liner will keep the rug, and you, from slipping. The second type is used when placing a rug on top of another soft surface such as carpet; it will keep an area rug from "creeping" across the room.

Similarly, it's important that wall-to-wall carpet is teamed with the right kind of pad. Various types and thicknesses are available; which one you choose will depend on the kind of carpet you have in the room. Supported by the right pad, your floor covering will not only last longer but also will have an extra layer of cushy comfort. An exception is integral-pad carpet; because it's bonded to a cushioned backing, there's no need for a separate pad.

# wood

● ● ● PART OF THE BEAUTY OF WOOD FLOORING is that it complements virtually any decor. It's equally at home in contemporary settings or in traditional rooms. Plus, this type of floor covering is easy to care for. There's a vast assortment of species available, from well-knowns such as maple, cherry, and oak to more exotic types such as rosewood, tigerwood, and zebrawood. If you're looking for something more rustic in nature—or a recycled option—consider a floor crafted from reclaimed lumber.

Because wood floors are susceptible to water, it's important that they be sealed. You'll find that most flooring found at your local home center is prefinished, but if you're installing a custom floor, you'll need to give it a sealer coat. Prefinished floors are good choices for rooms that use a single style throughout—a 3-in.-wide plank, for instance—but custom floors allow for more detailing, like an inlaid border.

**ABOVE** Some hardwood floors are bleached for simply aesthetic reasons to create a more aged or open and airy look. But there can also be a practical purpose; timeworn floors can be bleached to give them a new lease on life.

**RIGHT** Handsome hardwood floors run throughout this residence, the planks turned at right angles at each doorway to subtly define where one space transitions to the next.

A herringbone-patterned hardwood floor graces this foyer. Although the classic pattern is steeped in tradition, it partners equally well with modern elements like the stair runner and matching throw rug.

# ENGINEERED WOOD

f or floors that will get a lot of wear and tear, engineered-wood flooring can be a good alternative to conventional hardwood and it's easy to care for, too. Made up of a thin layer of wood veneer glued on top of plywood, this kind of flooring is less affected by moisture, more dimensionally stable, and can be installed more quickly than its counterpart. The cost, however, is comparable to solid wood.

Most engineered flooring—which is almost always prefinished—comes in tongue-and-groove strips, which must be stapled or glued to the subfloor. Some types, however, are designed for "floating" installations below grade, over concrete, or for any floor that is relatively level. Keep in mind, however, that the veneer layer of this flooring is typically only ¼ in. to ½ in. thick; only floors with the thickest veneers can be sanded and refinished.

The light hardwood floor in this city residence is right in step with the overall pale palette. A floor of darker oak or walnut would have weighed down the room, even distracted from the stunning view.

# painted wood floors

Paint, and a little pattern, can give wood floors a new lease on life. Maybe you have a less-than-perfect hardwood floor. Or you just want to express your creativity. Painted floors can be the solution to both situations, invariably giving you handsome results. Design options run the gamut from simple checkerboard patterns to stenciled images to elaborate trompe l'oeil effects. Before you go to all that effort, though, be sure that you use paint specially formulated for floor use. You can also use latex, as long as it's of a high quality. Just be sure, when finished, to protect your design with a coat of polyurethane.

**LEFT** Geometric motifs centered on the painted risers have the look of intricate marquetry at a fraction of the price. Applied with stencils, there's not a huge investment of time, either.

**BELOW** Painting the hardwood floor a creamy white provides a welcome contrast to the dark wood furnishings, allowing their silhouettes to stand out prominently. The high-gloss finish furthers the distinction, juxtaposing shiny and matte surfaces.

**ABOVE** This stairway takes an oft-neglected aspect—the risers—and turns them into eye-catching art. The various patterns are in no danger of wearing off, either, as this part of the floor doesn't get stepped on.

**LEFT** An oversize black-and-white checkerboard design gives this traditional foyer a modern twist. At the same time, the large pattern makes the area seem more spacious.

# laminate and vinyl

● ● ● RESILIENT FLOORING, WHICH INCLUDES VINYL and laminate, continues to be a popular option for rooms that get hard wear. Vinyl is particularly easy to maintain and is one of the least expensive floorings you'll find, available in sheet as well as tile forms.

Laminate flooring has a four-ply construction that consists of a backing, a moisture-resistant fiberboard, a decorative layer, and a tough "wear" layer on top. Laminates can take on the look of anything from wood to stone and for good reason: The decorative layer is an actual photograph. Laminates are highly durable as well as water and scratch resistant. What's more, this type of flooring—available in plank or tile form—can be installed on top of almost any kind of subfloor.

**BELOW** Vinyl has come a long way— today's offerings can replicate almost any type of floor covering. Case in point is the vinyl plank flooring in this kitchen. It offers the warmth and richness of hardwood at a fraction of the price of the real thing.

**ABOVE** One of the advantages of vinyl tiles lies in its versatility in terms of pattern. This kitchen sports a simple black-and-white checkerboard, but the possibilities are all but endless.

**Only upon close inspection can you tell that this floor is laminate and not true hardwood. Because this type of flooring is both scratch and water resistant, it's a good choice for a dining room.**

@ lthough it has an appearance that's often mistaken for wood, **bamboo** is actually a fast-growing grass. It's like wood in terms of hardness and comes in wide boards as well as narrow planks. You'll also find engineered and strand-woven types, both of which are created via a laminating process. And hand-scraped bamboo floors have an aged appearance, a little like reclaimed wood.

**Cork**, which has a honeycomb structure so it's about 50 percent air, is one of the most comfortable floorings you'll find. Plus, this kind of flooring—used in the work zone of many kitchens—deadens sound and acts as an insulator.

Not only is **rubber** durable, but what it offers in terms of aesthetics is impressive. Today's choices encompass a virtual rainbow of colors, and there's also a wide range of textures and patterns, including varieties that have the look of limestone or terrazzo.

# ceramic tile

● ● ● THE BEAUTY OF CERAMIC TILE IS THAT IT'S just as practical as it is eye-pleasing. From a functional point of view, it's durable and upkeep is easy. And, in terms of aesthetics, ceramic tile can infuse a room with virtually any color, pattern, or texture. There's versatility, too, in tile's sizes and shapes; floor tile can range from 1-in.-square mosaics all the way up to 16-in. by 16-in. squares.

For all its advantages, however, this type of floor covering has a downside. Ceramic tile tends to be noisy and isn't forgiving when something breakable, like a dish, is dropped on it. Plus, tile is cold underfoot unless radiant heat is installed beneath it. Still, the assets outweigh the drawbacks, which is why this flooring is always in vogue.

**Cream-colored surfaces envelope this bathroom, all smooth and sleek with the exception of one: Tiles with a pebble-like surface cross the floor, providing a more slip-resistant covering.**

Patterned ceramic tiles team up with their all-white companions in this kitchen, creating the look of an area rug beneath the room's central island.

# GREAT PRETENDERS

There was a time when if you wanted the look of stone, you had to install the real thing. Likewise, only lumber could provide the rich warmth of wood. That's not the case today—almost any flooring you choose can imitate several others. Ceramic tile can effect wood planks. Laminate flooring can look like stone. Even vinyl can take on the appearance of herringbone-patterned brick.

Thanks to these technological advancements, it's easier than ever to get the look you want at a price that will suit your budget in a material that will suit your lifestyle. Simply decide on your preferred look—whether it's wood or marble, brick or limestone—and then translate it to the type of flooring that best fits your overall needs.

Hardwood flooring in a bathroom can be problematic; the inherent humidity can take its toll. This master bath gets the best of both worlds; the ceramic tile floor is impervious to water and humidity and still provides the warm look of wood.

**ABOVE** By turning the black-and-white tiles in this foyer 90 degrees, instead of running them parallel to the walls, there's a greater feeling of movement in the room, inviting guests right into the house.

**RIGHT** Oversize tiles in this contemporary bathroom quietly make the room seem larger than its actual dimensions. The larger tiles have fewer grout lines breaking up the expanse, thus creating a more spacious feeling.

# MIXING
# MATERIALS

sing a mix of flooring materials in one space can do more than add unexpected visual interest. If a room has generous dimensions, for instance, using two types of flooring can help define separate spaces—such as living and dining areas. Likewise, a change in materials can create the look of an area rug; a "rug" made of ceramic tiles has the advantage of never slipping or creeping.

When combining different types of flooring, however, be sure that they are of similar heights. Too much of a step up or step down is likely to trip you up.

**The kitchen portion of this home's great room is underscored by patterned ceramic tiles, which provide some much-needed visual interest in a space filled with solid-wood cabinetry and all-white subway tiles.**

# stone, brick, and quarry tile

● ● ● HANDSOME STONE FLOORS HAVE THE KIND of versatility that makes them a good fit for any room. Marble tile can add elegance, while slate will have a more casual air. It's important to study the characteristics of each stone type; some varieties are practically indestructible, while others are vulnerable to scratches and cracks. Likewise, surface finishes can be just as varied as the kinds of stone themselves; tiles can be matte, polished, honed, antiqued, or even sandblasted.

Bricks and tiles made of natural clay are particularly appropriate for today's casual lifestyles. You can still find new handmade brick—its variations in color and texture all part of the charm—as well as those that have been salvaged. Machine-made varieties are also available, which are typically more uniform in size and color. Meanwhile, quarry tile comes in a wide range of shapes and sizes; although it's typically thought of as deep red in color, black and tan varieties are available, too.

**ABOVE** With its easygoing attitude, slate is suitable for casual spaces such as family rooms, but its hardworking nature makes it a good fit for kitchens and laundry rooms, too. Naturally stain and slip resistant, it comes in tile, slab, and mosaic form.

**LEFT** The red and yellow hues inherent to quarry tile provide instant warmth to a room. That can be advantageous in a kitchen, a space often filled with stainless steel appliances and surfaces.

# TILE SAFETY TIPS

Safety is a prime consideration when installing ceramic tile on the floor, particularly in water-prone rooms like kitchens and baths. The best precaution is to use slip-resistant tile. Every tile is given a coefficient of friction (COF) rating; these ratings range from 0 to 1, with tiles that have numbers of 0.6 and higher considered the most slip resistant.

Any rug placed on top of a tile floor should have the proper liner or, in the case of bathroom rugs, a rubber backing. Likewise, items such as small step stools should always have nonskid feet; this is particularly important in bathrooms used by small children, who need a step or two up to reach the sink.

**ABOVE** Rich marble tiles grace the foyer of this traditional home. Hexagonal shapes team up with squares here, creating a custom yet classic pattern. Stone is a particularly good choice for an entry as it can withstand years of wear and tear.

**RIGHT** A brick floor with a timeworn appearance—whether it's reclaimed or new tiles made to look old—adds a layer of casual warmth to a room, as evidenced in this country kitchen.

# storage

WHEN IT COMES TO CREATING AN ORGANIZED HOME, THERE ARE PLENTY OF attractive storage options. Multipurpose pieces such as chests, for instance, have the kind of flexibility that makes them good investments. A little-used chest in the guest room might be put to better use in the foyer, providing drawer storage for scarves and mittens. Likewise, if a remodeling project means you'll no longer be using an armoire as an entertainment center, move it to a bedroom for clothes storage.

That's not to say that there's not a place for storage pieces with specific purposes, too. The beauty of a china cabinet, for example, might be that it includes lighted shelves to show off your favorite patterns as well as drawers that will protect your best silverware.

Built-in storage also has its advantages. By taking inventory of your entertainment equipment—including CDs and DVDs—you can create a storage system to accommodate every piece. Likewise, take stock of your wardrobe before designing the ultimate walk-in closet. But built-ins don't have to be grand in scope to be great.

**A custom wall unit wrapped around a built-in credenza in this home office provides sufficient bookshelves for an entire library. The built-in not only offers enclosed storage for the nearby desk but an additional work surface, too.**

Build something as simple as a wine rack in the kitchen, where just the right bottle can always be conveniently close. Or you might add doors and drawers to otherwise wasted under-the-stairs space. With a little creativity, you can put every nook and cranny to good use.

# freestanding storage

● ● ● THE BEST THING ABOUT FREESTANDING storage is that it's portable, not only from one home to another but also from room to room. With the exception of a few specific-purpose pieces—bathroom vanities, for instance—most work just as well in one type of space as another. A sideboard, intended for the dining room, might make the move to a family room, housing picture albums, board games, or crafting essentials. And that toy box that your children used when they were young? Now that you're an empty-nester, why not use it for the toys of your "new child"—the dog?

A small freestanding storage piece may take its place quietly in a corner of a room, while a tall unit that stretches nearly to the ceiling can provide an eye-catching focal point. Some furnishings even provide two-sided storage, while others have backs finished in such fine detail that they can make handsome room dividers.

More and more, fine furniture—like this handsome vanity—is finding its way into the bathroom. The warm wood finish is a welcome addition to a space that can sometimes seem cold.

Think beyond conventional labels; there's no need to reserve a china cabinet for the dining room only. In this living room, the traditional piece showcases books and prized possessions behind its glass doors.

**ABOVE** The statuesque armoire in this living room is just as fashionable as it is functional, its dramatic design providing an eye-catching focal point in the otherwise subdued scheme.

**LEFT** The undisputed star of this dining room is an antique painted cupboard, its contrasting dark interior the perfect foil for a treasured collection of silver and creamware.

# • chests and cabinets

**The appeal of a simple storage piece like this is that it's right at home anywhere. The straightforward design partners just as easily with contemporary furnishings as it does with traditional styles.**

The beauty of chests and cabinets goes far beyond their hardworking nature. Available in every imaginable style, they can blend beautifully into your decor or serve as a completely unexpected counterpoint. A classic highboy, for instance, can be right at home in a traditional bedroom. The same piece, however, might be a stunning addition to an all-white, contemporary surround, taking on sculptural status against the canvas-like backdrop.

You'll find that the most versatile pieces are those that feature styling that is both simple and understated; minimal ornamentation gives chests and cabinets a chameleon-like quality, making them right at home almost anywhere. That said, a highly decorated model—with a decorative paint finish or ornamental shells—may be just the thing to take your room from ordinary into the realm of extraordinary.

**ABOVE** An antique vault safely stores dinnerware in this dining room, while serving as a conversation piece, too. What's more, the repurposed piece is right in step with being green.

**BELOW** This traditional storage piece lends an air of formality to the room. But its multiple drawers, graduated in size, can quietly house anything—even children's toys and games.

t oday's varied choices in home electronics translate to an equally wide array of storage systems. To determine what entertainment center will best suit your needs, start by taking stock of the equipment you have. Make a list of the major components as well as their dimensions, including your television, DVD player, speakers—anything that takes up physical space. Next, compile all of your CDs, DVDs, and the like, and then measure them to find out how many linear feet of storage space they'll require.

Once you've come up with a number, estimate how much more space you'll need as your collection grows. Only after you've done the math—armed with your room's dimensions as well as your specific storage needs—will you be ready to shop wisely for a home entertainment unit.

The advent of flat-screen TVs has allowed entertainment units to downsize accordingly. Today, a TV and all of its accompanying components can fit easily in small-scale units like this decorative piece.

**ABOVE** What makes this traditional huntboard well suited to the stair landing is its long legs. A solid chest would have taken up more visual space, appearing too large for the small area.

**RIGHT** Armoires, like this French example, originally housed suits of armor. Today, they're some of the most versatile storage pieces you'll find, accommodating everything from clothes and accessories to toys, games, and televisions.

A country-style cupboard may, at first, seem a mismatch for an otherwise refined, traditional room. In fact, the piece has classic lines in common with the rest of the furnishings, allowing it to blend beautifully into the room.

# SHELVING UNITS

t here's nothing quite so accommodating as a simple shelf unit. This is storage in its most basic form, ready to serve a purely functional purpose or support more decorative endeavors. Some may be little tuck-away pieces that sit discreetly in a corner of a room; small versions, for instance, might hold towels in the bathroom or be devoted to treasured volumes of books. Taller ones, with their extended vertical reach, might hold collectibles. Pieces that are open from front to back make storage easily accessible from either side and, if large enough, can be good room dividers, too— particularly appealing for those living in loft-style spaces.

Don't forget about wall-hung shelving options, either. Plate racks are one of the most common options, but there are all kinds of custom alternatives. Shelves supported by adjustable brackets, for example, can provide custom storage in a matter of minutes.

As if it were made specifically for this powder room, the decorative top of this wall-hung shelving unit echoes the swag motif found in the wallpaper. Here, the shelves display artfully arranged flowers, but they could just as easily hold bathroom essentials such as soaps and hand towels.

The beauty of wall-hung shelving modules is that they can be arranged in countless configurations to fit the size and shape of your available space.

# •china cabinets, sideboards, and buffets

Storage pieces specific to dining rooms—china cabinets, sideboards, and buffets—will serve you best if, before buying, you take stock of what needs to be housed. Take inventory of your dinnerware, allowing for those pieces that you still want to purchase, including china, silverware, stemware, and serving pieces.

With glass doors and interior lighting, a china cabinet can be a stunning showcase for your favorite pieces. Some lights are operated with simple switches, while others have stepped-up levels of illumination controlled by a mere touch of special hinges. Meanwhile, buffets and sideboards are similar in size and shape and have a common purpose; not only do they provide storage space within but also good-sized serving areas on top.

**Intricate fretwork immediately draws your eye to this fine china cabinet. Behind the glass-fronted doors, however, a coral-colored interior gives the traditional storage piece a fresh, modern-day twist.**

**TOP LEFT** In this dining room, a Mid-Century Modern sideboard features a niche just the right size to keep an entire coffee service at the ready. Storage pieces that offer open storage let you keep most-used items conveniently close.

**LEFT** Three-dimensional faceting on the front of the credenza catches the light from different angles, creating an ever-changing artistic effect that's appropriately framed by the dark-wood surround.

**ABOVE** If space is at a premium in the dining room, consider a small-scale server. This one, with drawers, is just big enough to hold a set of flatware; when a buffet is being served, the hinged top extends to double the surface dimensions.

A pair of traditional nightstands flank this bed, their dark frames not only offering a welcome contrast against the cream-colored upholstered bed and matching linens but also visually anchoring the sleeping spot.

# •dressers and nightstands

Triple dressers have long been a common-sense storage solution; with three small drawers along the top and larger drawers below, they provide a good his-and-hers option. They do, however, measure about 76 in. long, making them too large for some of today's scaled-down spaces. One alternative is to use a chest that's taller than it is wide. Or opt for a pair of more diminutive bachelor's chests, placing each where it's most convenient for the user.

Nightstands provide another good opportunity for storage while keeping bedside necessities close at hand. Historically, two-drawer models have been most popular, but today designs vary as much as personal style. Small dressers, chests, and even desks can substitute for conventional nightstands, too, as long as they're no more than 2 in. higher or lower than the top of the bed's mattress.

# QUALITY CHECKPOINTS
# FOR DOORS AND DRAWERS

**W**ell-made doors and drawers are the hallmarks of any good storage piece. It's easy to distinguish the best ones. Before making a purchase, look for these indicators of quality:

**Doors:**

• Doors should hang evenly and swing with ease; latches should also operate smoothly.

• All hinges should be firmly attached. If exterior hinges are screwed on, the screws should go all the way through the door as well as the furniture frame and be secured with a nut on the opposite side.

**Drawers:**

• Look for dovetail joints; drawers put together with nails, screws, or glue are not as stable.

• Drawers should open and close easily. Center glides are necessary on larger drawers for stability, keeping them from wobbling from side to side. Drawer stops are important, as well, to prevent drawers from sliding all the way out when you open them.

• Be sure that drawer interiors are smoothly sanded; rough surfaces are more likely to snag items, such as delicate clothing.

**ABOVE** A bachelor's chest takes on double-duty in this bedroom. Its marble top has more than sufficient space for bedside necessities with plenty of room for clothes storage in the drawers below.

**LEFT** Making the most of every square inch of space, this bedroom foregoes a conventional dresser in lieu of a one-of-a-kind antique secretary. There's plenty of storage for clothing plus a drop-lid desk for catching up on correspondence.

An industrial-style island gives this kitchen much of its laid-back attitude, with open shelving that makes it easy to access everyday items. Because it's on casters, the island can easily be moved, too, perhaps closer to a counter when extra workspace is needed.

# • special-purpose pieces

More than ever, furniture pieces are making their way into the kitchen and bath, providing specialized storage. In the kitchen, for instance, an island no longer needs to be site built. You'll find a wide array of freestanding furnishings that not only provide additional workspace but convenient storage, too. For the bath, there are all kinds of open and closed storage options to keep towels and toiletries close at hand, from the smallest two-tier shelf to grand vanities that are just as fashionable as they are functional.

**ABOVE** Taking advantage of every square inch of vertical space, this storage piece features shelves that keep linens accessible with drawers below for all manner of bathroom necessities. Its straightforward styling, though, makes it a good candidate for almost any room.

**ABOVE** An island lends continuity to this cheery kitchen, painted the same bright white as the cabinetry. Its butcher-block top is a smart choice, too, providing an eating area that doubles as a chopping board.

**LEFT** A chest is smartly repurposed in this master bath, retrofitted with a sink and fittings set into a new marble top. Even after allowing room for the necessary plumbing, some of the drawer space is still usable.

# built-ins

●●● BUILT-INS ARE GREAT BECAUSE THEY UTILIZE every square inch of potential storage space. They can span a wall from floor to ceiling or simply carve out a bookshelf under a window seat. In short, built-ins can transform even the oddest nook or cranny into a hardworking storage area.

The real beauty of built-ins is that they can be custom tailored, not only to your specific needs but also your personal style. There's typically more time and expense involved than with freestanding pieces, but there's usually a long-term benefit: Built-ins can be an attractive selling point for your home when the time comes. Keep in mind, however, that this type of storage often requires a professional contractor, especially if it's elaborate.

Custom cabinetry along one wall of this living room is as crisp and well tailored as the rest of the room's furnishings, providing the right mix of open and closed storage to accommodate everything from artwork to electronics.

**ABOVE** The top bunk in this boy's room is accessed via steps, which provide an opportunity for storage, too. Folded clothing fits easily into these drawers, but they could just as easily hold toys and games.

**LEFT** Consider all of the possibilities when carving out storage. In this sitting room, least-used books are stashed on shelves at ceiling level; when needed, they can be retrieved with the help of a rolling library ladder.

# •entries and hallways

The potential for entries and hallways goes beyond playing the roles of traffic directors and pass-throughs. Some of the most inconspicuous nooks and crannies can be put to work as storage space. A mere sliver of space inside the door, for instance, might be designated for a built-in bench, not only providing a spot to sit while pulling on boots but—with space carved out below—a place to store them, too.

In central hallways, look for opportunities to carve out room to stash often-used items like vacuums and cleaning supplies. Unused spaces under stairways work well for the same purpose, but these areas can also be outfitted with any combination of open and closed storage. Think of them as great out-of-the way places for books, toys and games, even bed linens for a nearby sleeper sofa.

**Once no more than a square box of a space, this mudroom is now fitted with a custom closet flanked by benches with drawer storage beneath. The closet, which stretches all the way to the ceiling, visually breaks up what could have seemed like a cavernous room.**

# LOCKER-STYLE STORAGE

there's a reason that lockers are popular in school hallways—they can stash all kinds of personal belongings in a relatively small space. So why not adapt them to the home? Locker-style storage inside your back door can instantly organize each member of the family. A top shelf can be designated for hats and mittens and the bottom for boots. And there's still plenty of space in between to hang coats and store everything from baseball bats to umbrellas.

This type of storage lends itself just as easily to built-ins as it does freestanding forms; just be sure that the latter are secured to the wall. To make it easy on yourself, coat the lockers with tough-as-nails paint, one that will easily wipe clean.

**ABOVE** Built-in storage at this landing takes on a locker-style appearance. To utilize every square inch of available space, drawers below the tall doors stair-step accordingly.

**ABOVE** At one end of this built-in, locker-style units provide a place to hang coats, with baskets above for hats and gloves, and below for boots and shoes. Meanwhile, a bench to one side offers a place to sit while getting ready to go outdoors, with even more storage below.

**ABOVE** All of the traditional attributes of locker-style storage are present in this mudroom. Because the built-in is crafted of the same contemporary elements as the rest of the room, it blends seamlessly into the space.

**ABOVE** Locker-style storage flanks a window in this child's room, with easily accessible open storage below. Because the locker units stretch all the way to the ceiling, the window seat between them feels even cozier.

# •living and dining areas

**With built-in floor-to-ceiling bookshelves surrounding this space, it's a bibliophile's dream. The dark wood shelves are contrasted by the same bright white trim used throughout the room, framing them beautifully in the process.**

The kind of lifestyle you lead will determine the type—and amount—of storage space that you need in living and dining areas. If you entertain formally on a regular basis, you may want a built-in bar in the living room that can house everything from glasses and stemware to small cutting boards and cocktail napkins. More informal areas, like family rooms, inevitably need designated space for home electronics and their various accessories;

young families will put a premium on plenty of space for toys and games.

As for the dining room, think beyond the requisite storage for dinnerware to other needs you may have. If you don't have the luxury of a home office, for instance, incorporate a small desk surface into built-in storage, a place where you can set your laptop. Plus, it can double as a serving spot.

**LEFT** The clean-lined styling of this hutch makes it just as modern as the rest of the room's furnishings. On a day-to-day basis, the built-in niche accommodates collectibles as well as bar essentials, but it can also serve up a meal buffet-style at a moment's notice.

**BELOW** A storage wall in this dining room stops just short of the ceiling, allowing light to filter in from windows in the adjacent space. The bank of symmetrical drawer storage creates a sense of tranquility, too.

In this open floor plan, a single space has to serve several purposes: It's a relaxing reading spot, a place to watch TV, and a home office, too. Still, there's a sense of continuity because the essentials for all are housed within the same natural-finished shelves.

# tv storage

If your home electronics consist of little more than a TV and DVD player, a small cabinet or small armoire may be all you need to safely house the equipment—even a low-profile unit that can hold a flat-screen TV on top (or it may be mounted on the wall above) and other electronics below could fit the bill. On the other hand, if you have an extensive audio/video system, modular storage may be a better solution. You'll find designs ranging from classic traditional to ultra-contemporary that can accommodate all the sizes and shapes of today's TVs. Plus, there are niches and nooks for every imaginable accessory, including game consoles and sound docking systems.

To take TV storage to the nth degree, though, consider custom built-in units. You'll be able to accommodate all of your equipment without wasting an inch of space.

The center section of this built-in storage unit perfectly accommodates a large flat-screen TV. Instead of trying to disguise it, the owners opted to frame the television, giving it even more importance.

**ABOVE** In keeping with the casual theme of the room, barn-style doors conceal a large flat-screen TV. When it's time to watch a favorite program, the doors simply slide to each side.

**LEFT** Decorative fronts on these storage doors artfully conceal a flat-screen TV, with plenty of room left over for everything from books to board games. Push latches make the doors easy to open and don't interrupt their geometric design.

# • kitchens

**A sliver of space at one end of the breakfast table is as hardworking as the rest of the kitchen, providing a place to stash cookbooks and collectibles, even a small wine collection.**

In the kitchen, cabinetry is the most obvious type of built-in storage. Take stock of your cooking habits and your personal style, and then come up with the right combination of wall and base cabinetry, including shelves, racks, and bins. Be sure to think beyond the conventional configuration of wall cabinets over base models and standard drawers over doors. You may be surprised to find that basic components can be configured to look like freestanding, finely detailed pieces of furniture.

To make your kitchen even more efficient, you may want to incorporate a mini-office, too—especially if you don't have a designated home office. With room enough for a laptop, it can be the perfect place to pay bills, plan menus, or for the kids to do homework.

Built-in banquette seating is a space-saver in its own right, but this example takes efficiency to the next level by incorporating under-the-bench drawer storage.

# more about...
# DRAWER PULLS

**W**ith a small investment, and even less time, new knobs and pulls can give cabinetry a fresh look. There are glass versions with a vintage look, metal renditions that look like twigs and leaves, and designs that reflect virtually any penchant or personal style.

If you're replacing a knob, which attaches with a single screw, be sure that the screw on the new piece of hardware is similar in size to the old one. (If necessary, you can make the hole in the door or drawer larger, though you can't make it smaller.) Likewise, if you're switching out pulls—attached with two screws—be sure that the distance between the two holes is the same on the new piece as the one you're replacing.

One corner of this kitchen is dedicated to a home office, its work surface consisting of the same marble used for countertops throughout the room. Tall cabinet doors are fronted with see-through fabric instead of solid wood to keep the storage wall from appearing too imposing.

# •baths

Bathrooms have long since moved out of the realm of mere utilitarian spaces. Today, they're more apt to be personal spas, and built-in storage plays a big role in creating these luxurious rooms. Integral elements can run the gamut from simple to sophisticated, from the most basic wall hooks and pegs to well-outfitted linen closets. To determine what kinds of storage best suits your lifestyle, give some thought to who uses the room and when. Do you and your spouse get ready for work at the same time? If so, a double vanity is probably in order, with plenty of space for each person's grooming essentials. Does one of you shower while the other one bathes? Then consider some kind of towel storage between the two spots.

A wall of fine wood cabinetry anchors the master bath, long enough to accommodate twin vanities. Mirroring all of the upper cabinets is not only functional; it also bounces light back into the space, making it seem brighter, and keeps the dark wood from overpowering the otherwise white space.

**ABOVE** Open shelves tucked into a niche in this bathroom make everything on them easily accessible. There's even room for a small TV; viewable from the tub, it adds another layer of luxury to the room.

**TOP RIGHT** In this bath, a contemporary cabinet and vanity take on a sculptural appearance, their rectangular shapes balanced by a simple round mirror. Because the storage pieces are wall-hung, they take up less visual and physical space—a good strategy for any small space.

**ABOVE** What could have been a bath with straightforward style—a pair of square vanities with a tall cabinet between them—is infused with fun, thanks to the cabinet's light-and-dark angled drawers and a mirrored door panel that echoes the asymmetrical shapes.

# •bedrooms

Built-ins make perfect sense in a bedroom, whether the space is large or small. On one hand, if a room's dimensions are spacious, there are multiple options. You may opt to create a wall of storage opposite the bed, with room enough not only for clothing but also a TV and other home electronic equipment. Or you might use built-ins to subdivide a long and narrow space into two distinct areas—one for sleeping and the other a quiet conversation area. The storage can reach to the ceiling or just halfway up; either way, both sides can be fitted with doors, drawers, and shelves.

But built-ins are good candidates for small rooms, too. In lieu of a conventional headboard and two night tables, for instance, flank the bed with to-the-ceiling cabinetry that can store everything from clothing to bedside essentials.

**Built-in storage makes sense in an under-the-eaves bedroom, where the ceiling may not be tall enough for freestanding pieces. Built-ins make the best use of this small space, providing a wardrobe, a nightstand, even drawers under the bed.**

A streamlined storage wall in this bedroom seems even more so because there is no hardware visually interrupting it. Instead, touch-latch hardware was used to keep the look clean.

## more about...
# KIDS' STORAGE

t he key to storage in kids' rooms is versatility. Not only do built-in units need to accommodate their current possessions, but the pieces should be able to adapt to future needs, too. A conventional storage wall—with open shelves above and closed doors below— might hold books and toys, respectively, for a toddler. In teen years, the same storage system could just as easily house sports paraphernalia and home electronics.

In kids' rooms especially, safety must come into play. Doors should be designed so they won't snap shut on small fingers or, depending on what's behind them, even have kid-proof latches. Or opt for open shelves fitted with baskets and bins. As long as they're at a child's eye level or below, lightweight containers can safely be pulled out and put back again.

In this child's room, basic white shelf units get a custom touch. Both are topped with "crowns" that are whimsical in their shapes and colors. Best of all, they can be created with not much more than plywood and paint.

What could have been an ordinary built-in storage unit crosses into the realm of extraordinary, thanks to a shapely cornice at the top of the piece and creatively applied coats of paint.

# • mudrooms and laundry areas

Just because they're some of the hardest-working rooms in the home doesn't mean they can't have substance and style, too. For the most part, mudrooms and utility areas simply need easy-care areas at their core. Start by evaluating your family's needs, then create built-in storage around them. Do one or two adults regularly pass through the mudroom, or is it constantly trafficked by kids? The former may need nothing more than a couple of coat hooks and a boot rack, while the latter might require individually assigned lockers. Likewise, in the laundry room, consider how many loads you do a week, then provide ample storage space for sorting bins and detergents as well as the ironing board.

**A few basic elements combine to create the look of towering furniture in this mudroom. Open-shelf units provide storage as well as bench seating, while simple paneling and a row of coat hooks span the space between.**

**LEFT** Today's stacking appliances make it possible to tuck a washer and dryer—plus a sink—in an area the size of a double closet. A few feet of adjacent space is carved out here, making room for pull-out drawers that hold everyday necessities.

**LEFT AND ABOVE** Casting a glance around this room, there's no clue that—behind an unassuming set of cabinet doors—a full-size washer and dryer let the owner keep laundry going without ever leaving the kitchen.

# lighting

THE RIGHT LIGHT IN A ROOM CAN HAVE A DRAMATIC DECORATIVE IMPACT. A pendant lamp shining down on a polished granite surface, for instance, can add instant sparkle to a space. Likewise, a well-placed spotlight can add depth and dimension to a painting on the wall.

Many fixtures themselves are aesthetically appealing but—before making your choice—be sure that it will fulfill its intended role. All three types of lighting—general, task, and accent—should, typically, be represented in a room. General lighting might come from a bank of recessed fixtures or a striking chandelier. Task lighting can consist of pendants in the kitchen or a reading lamp next to your favorite chair. And accent lighting may be provided by a sconce that, with its upward beam, decoratively washes a wall with light.

When selecting a light fixture for a room, keep in mind what time of day you'll be using it; that will make a difference as to how bright—or not—the light source will need to be. Keep in mind, too, that some lights cast a warm glow, while others have a cooler nature.

A good lighting plan is integral to any good decorating scheme and not a mere afterthought. If you're building or remodeling, take full advantage of the situation; by establishing a lighting plan early on, you can provide the right wiring for any type of fixture.

**A combination of recessed and pendant lighting safely illuminates the kitchen for any task at hand. But because the recessed lights at ceiling level are tucked into rectangular cutouts, there's an artistic effect, too.**

# general lighting

● ● ● JUST AS ITS NAME IMPLIES, GENERAL— or ambient—lighting provides a soft, overall glow. In the kitchen, for instance, recessed canisters can illuminate the entire room. At its most basic level, this type of lighting allows you to walk through a room without tripping over the kids' toys. But it's only the starting point for any lighting scheme. Once a room's general lighting is in place, you can concentrate on illuminating specific areas with task and accent lighting.

In addition to canisters, there are other types of recessed lighting that can provide general lighting. Or, there's a wealth of more decorative options; a single chandelier or several pendant lamps can provide the necessary light while complementing your decor. Even strategically placed table and floor lamps can supply a sufficient amount of ambient lighting. The bottom line is this: Whatever type you choose to use, be sure that it's distributed evenly throughout the room.

**A single, oversize pendant is often used over a dining table, but in this kitchen three of the fixtures line up to shed light on an entire island. The dark brown shades are a natural, too, echoing the hue of the ceiling beams.**

A pair of chandeliers in this dining area shed light in an understated way; their see-through glass shades in no way block, or even detract from, the stunning view just beyond the windows.

## A BALANCED APPROACH

e ach room requires a mix of the three basic types of lighting—general, task, and accent. When the balance is just right, there's enough illumination for every need; you can walk through a room and see where you are going, work at the computer without straining your eyes, *and* showcase that special work of art.

But this three-prong approach is more than merely functional. With table and floor lamps at eye level, sconces higher on the wall, and chandeliers hanging overhead, a well-lit room creates visually interesting areas of shadow and light. Think of it like a painting that's infinitely more interesting with a variety of values than if everything were the exact same intensity.

This room's general lighting is enhanced by task lighting—wall-hung lamps in the alcove that make for easy reading—as well as accent lighting, comprising recessed spots in the same alcove and directional lights that showcase books and collectibles.

**ABOVE** A rectangular fixture replicates the shape of the kitchen island, assuring that every square inch of the workspace below is sufficiently lit. Because the two elements are nearly the same color, there's a soothing sense of continuity, as well.

**RIGHT** In a kitchen full of sharp angles—found in the island, the cabinetry, even the appliances—a trio of glass fixtures with softly curved shapes lend equilibrium to the overall look.

# DIMMERS AND TIMERS

d immer switches are a surefire way to add instant drama to any room. They're easy to install and inexpensive, too. First, though, be sure that your light is a candidate for a dimmer switch. As a general rule, fluorescents and halogens are not good options, nor are three-way switches. When choosing a dimmer—available in toggle, dial, and touch-sensitive styles—be sure to select one that's rated to handle the total wattage of the lights it will control.

Like dimmers, timers help control how much light is used. Manual timers—those that plug into wall outlets on one side and the fixtures they control on the other—are, perhaps, best known. But technology has advanced these lighting add-ons. You'll also find programmable timers in the form of wall switches that can control multiple lights.

**TOP LEFT** The metal-and-glass light fixture used in this outdoor dining area is durable enough to withstand the elements but at the same time makes a dramatic statement, mirroring the shape of the table below.

**LEFT** Dark wood cabinetry wraps this city kitchen, even fronting the appliances so all stay quietly in the background. The demure setting gives a pair of red pendants even more prominence, while surrounding track lights lithely dance around the fixtures.

During the day, a skylight centered over this kitchen's marble island floods the space with natural light. Evenly spaced recessed fixtures augment the skylight by day or provide dramatic lighting on their own by night.

# g a l l e r y

## chandeliers

Chandeliers have traditionally been a good choice for the dining room, casting a soft glow over the table. More and more, however, chandeliers are showing up throughout the house, providing general illumination in the foyer, the living room, even the kitchen and bath. And they've long since shed their purely formal reputations; today's offerings run the style gamut.

As a general rule, the fixture should be positioned so the bottom is approximately 30 in. above the surface that it illuminates. When the height of the room is more than 8 ft., though, raise the height 2 in. to 3 in. per extra foot for better visual balance.

**ABOVE** A chandelier in this dining room is encircled by a drum shade, giving the fixture a more casual feeling that's in keeping with the room itself.

**ABOVE** In this casual dining area, the chandelier is a work of art in its own right, with the familiar candelabra bulbs peeking out amidst white-painted twigs.

**TOP LEFT** Ensconced in a brass-and-glass globe, the chandelier's round shape is a welcome contrast to the rectangular forms throughout the rest of the room.

**LEFT** The arms of this chandelier dip below its shade, echoing its curved shapes in the process. The shorter shade also allows light from the fixture to spread more broadly across the area.

# task lighting

● ● ● TASK LIGHTING CAN TAKE VARIOUS FORMS— from table and floor lamps to pendants and wall fixtures. But the focus is always precisely the same. Whether you're reading a book or working at the computer, this type of light will give you a clearer picture of the task at hand. Generally, lights fitted with soft white bulbs (as opposed to clear) are easier on the eyes. Above all, however, it's important that task lighting illuminate evenly, without creating any shadows or glare.

Lamps and fixtures with cone-shaped shades are one of the best options for task lighting because they create a wide pool of light. Or, you might opt for a drum shade that has equal-size openings at the top and bottom; it can serve double duty, shedding light on the intended task and reflecting ambient light off the ceiling, too.

**Flexible-arm lamps are often seen on desktops, but wall-hung versions—which can be turned at various angles and moved back and forth—work beautifully over the vanity in this bathroom.**

**In a dark room, like this home office with deep green walls and coral shelves, lamps with light shades are best bets to illuminate surfaces and brighten the space.**

A wide variety of objects—from toy drums to teapots—can be wired to create one-of-a-kind lamps. A found piece of driftwood provided the starting point for this table lamp, apropos for the eclectic bedroom.

An adjustable base on the floor lamp allows it to be raised and lowered with ease, bringing the light source as close as need be to the task at hand.

# LIGHT BULBS

today's light bulbs vary almost as much as today's lighting fixtures, each with its own distinct glow. Some of the most common types are:

- **Incandescent:** The most familiar type of light bulb, incandescents cast a warm, soft glow. Though not the most efficient—only 10 percent of their energy produces light while 90 percent is radiated as heat—incandescents are inexpensive and work well with dimmers.

- **Halogen:** Halogen bulbs emit a clear white light, casting "true" light on the items around them. While they are more energy efficient than incandescents, they can also get very hot, even creating a fire hazard. A variation on halogen is the xenon bulb; it not only burns cooler but also uses even less energy.

- **Fluorescent:** Fluorescents are not only one of the most energy-efficient options, but they also come in a variety of colors, even matching the warm glow of incandescents.

- **Compact fluorescent light bulbs:** These bulbs, commonly known as CFLs, are basically small fluorescent tubes that have been folded over so they fit into sockets designed for incandescent bulbs. CFLs cost more but save money in the long run because they use only one-quarter the energy of incandescent bulbs and last approximately 10 times longer.

- **LED bulbs:** Although initially more expensive, these bulbs offer long-term advantages. They use approximately 85 percent less energy than incandescents and can last up to 20 years longer.

The beauty of this three-arm floor lamp lies not only in its dramatic silhouette. Its multiple light sources can all be focused on the same surface or on separate ones.

ABOVE  The lighting solution for this country-style bath couldn't be simpler. A trio of silver-bowl bulbs illuminate the sink, the metallic tips redirecting light back toward the wall and not in someone's face.

ABOVE  Against a white wall this lamp would have been lost, but its shapely form is showcased beautifully against the room's dark walls, making it nearly as important an art element as the modern painting next to it.

## SIMPLE SCONCES

If you have sufficient task lighting in a bath or powder room, sconces on either side of a mirror can take a strictly decorative tack. These primitive metal versions support nothing more than standard candles that cast a soft glow over the room. The candles can easily be replaced at any time, or rechargeable lights that look like candles could be used here. In addition to its decorative appeal, this solution has other merits. Because no hard wiring is required, electrical costs are lower.

Primitive sconces fitted with standard candles are a perfect fit for this rustic-chic bathroom. The metal fixtures are just as unassuming as the vanity below.

# accent lighting

● ● ● ACCENT LIGHTING HAS THE POTENTIAL TO ADD visual excitement to any room. It can be used, for instance, to highlight spectacular works of art or architectural elements. Spotlights and track lights are particularly good for this purpose because their beams can be aimed at specific objects.

This type of lighting can also bathe a feature wall—perhaps one with a decorative finish—in a dramatic way. Track or recessed lights installed on the ceiling, approximately 2 ft. to 3 ft. from the wall, can all be angled in the same direction to evenly wash a wall in light. Decorative wall sconces also fall into the category of accent light. But no matter what type of light you use, there is a single formula to follow: Accent lighting should always be at least three times brighter than the ambient lighting of a room so the object it's showcasing shines just a little brighter.

A pair of sconces over the fireplace draw the eye to the architectural focal point of the room and, at the same time, beautifully showcase the artwork atop the mantel.

t rack lighting has come a long way since the days when matching lights were mounted at equidistant intervals. The lights mounted along a track can still be changed and rearranged, added or deleted. Today, however, you can use a mix of styles along a single track or even change the type of light entirely—from incandescent to high-intensity halogen and back again, depending on each one's purpose.

Likewise, tracks are no longer all perfectly straight; some are flexible, allowing you to twist and turn however you see fit. Plus, not all lights need to be attached directly to the track itself. Some lightweight models are suspended from their tracks with nothing more than a thin wire.

**ABOVE** The way in which this fixture sheds its light makes it an impressive accent in the room. Rays of light and shadow encircle it, emulating the feeling of sunshine.

**RIGHT** Sconces that shed light both up and down have the ability to beautifully illuminate an accent wall. The chrome finish of these contemporary fixtures blends quietly with the weathered-wood wall.

Picture lights need not be reserved for works of art. In this living room, a row of brass picture lights illuminates an entire library wall.

**LEFT** The style of this sconce accents the foyer as much as the light source itself. The fixture, with its dramatic black shade and curlicue brass base, takes on a three-dimensional sculptural effect.

**BELOW** A treasured collection of woven baskets gets the spotlight on this shelf, thanks to individual fixtures that can be adjusted to pinpoint beams precisely where they're needed.

# finishing touches

• • •

DECORATING A ROOM BUT STOPPING SHORT OF ACCESSORIES IS LIKE running a race and not completing the last mile. The right accents—which can include everything from fine art to quirky collectibles—are just as important to a scheme as the furniture, the flooring, and the window and wall coverings. These finishing touches can follow the lead of your decorative style; in a primitive country bedroom, for instance, a stack of colorful Shaker-style boxes is a perfect fit. Likewise, in a contemporary space, an avant-garde work of art reflects a penchant for modern design.

Just as important, accessories provide the single best opportunity to surround yourself with the things you love, those items that give you comfort. A traditionalist might fill a mantel with ancestral photographs, while a free spirit might put a collection of antique lunch boxes on display.

That's not to imply that decorative accessories throughout your house need to be of the same style, type, or even vintage. In fact, it's much more visually appealing to mix old and new, fine objects with found items, hand-me-downs with newly purchased pieces. From time to time, change your perspective by changing and rearranging things; items you've had for years will take on a fresh look. Likewise, go "shopping" in your own home from time to time. You may be surprised to discover long-forgotten treasures that will blend into your scheme beautifully.

**The right finishing touches can transform an ordinary room into something extraordinary. Atop this bedside table, for instance, a rich purple vase and matching water carafe bring an unexpected pop of color into the space.**

# wall decor

•  •  • TODAY'S APPROACH TO WALL DECOR IS more eclectic than ever before. While some people prefer to hang fine paintings in their homes in gallery-like fashion, others are more inclined to let their imaginations run wild, showcasing everything from vintage maps to garden gates. In fact, anything that can be supported by a nail in the wall presents an opportunity for an artistic wall accent.

And what if the objects of your desire don't lend themselves to being hung on the wall? Custom-built shelves can play a supporting role. Use one alone or stack several—whether in perfect vertical rows or barely overlapping one another. In contemporary settings, you might also consider three-dimensional cubes in lieu of standard shelves. Not only can they provide a dramatic place to display collectibles, but they also become an inherent part of the room's architecture.

Even the most utilitarian items can have a sculptural effect. In this clean-lined kitchen, there's an artistic quality to the simple shelves lined with stark white dishes.

A wall-hung heirloom quilt provides a welcome splash of color and pattern in an otherwise subdued country-style room. Soft furnishings like this can easily be swapped out, as well, to create another scheme entirely.

**ABOVE** The large mirror in this dining room could have easily overwhelmed a single photograph on the adjacent wall. But by amassing three photos—and enlarging the group further with a few well-placed starfish—there's a much greater sense of equilibrium.

**LEFT** In this powder room, a mirror encircled by slats from old wine barrels replicates the look of a decorative sunburst while staying right in step with the rest of the bath's rustic-chic pieces.

The large black-and-white aerial map that overlooks the sofa would have been impressive enough had it been left intact. But by sectioning it, giving each a black frame, the drama is multiplied accordingly.

# •pictures and prints

Arranging pictures and prints—like the pieces themselves—is largely a matter of personal preference. Still, there are some guidelines that will allow you to appreciate each to its utmost. Large works intended to stand alone should be given a place of prominence, over the fireplace, for instance, or as a focal point at the end of a hall. The smaller the pieces are, however, the more flexibility you have.

A single painting might be placed over a desk, where it's in plain view each time you sit down to work. Or, you might give several pieces more emphasis by grouping them together. Even if they don't have similar subjects, you can create continuity by using matching mats and frames.

**FACING PAGE TOP** There's no hard-and-fast rule that pictures and prints—or mirrors, for that matter—must be hung on a wall. An assemblage is propped atop a bookcase in this living room, in keeping with its casual character.

**FACING PAGE BOTTOM** Photographs of the owners' favorite places create a sure conversation starter in this family room. Matted and framed similarly, the unrelated images work together beautifully as a whole.

## more about...
# HANGING ART

**c**omposing a wall grouping doesn't have to be an overwhelming prospect. Simply arrange the elements on a tabletop or floor first, then transpose them to the intended wall. Start with brown kraft paper that's slightly larger than your finished grouping. Put it on a flat surface, and then play with the composition of your arrangement. It's a good idea to establish one strong horizontal line and, if possible, a vertical line, too. Keep moving the pieces around, balancing heavy and light—from both physical and visual points of view—while keeping spacing equidistant.

Once you're satisfied with the arrangement, mark where the nail holes for each piece should be. Then, with painter's tape, attach the kraft paper to the wall. (For an over-the-sofa grouping, hang the bottom pieces low enough so there's a visual link to the piece of furniture but not so low that you'll hit your head against them.) Drive nails and/or hangers into the appropriate places, and then remove the paper from the wall. If wall anchors are needed, determine their positions on the paper, but don't install them until after the paper's been removed. After the nails, hangers, and anchors are in place, all that's left to do is hang the individual pieces—then stand back and admire them.

What makes this group of Audubon prints impressive is the sheer number as much as the imagery itself. Multiple works invariably increase the dramatic impact, whether the content is original or prints taken from the pages of a book.

# gallery

## think in 3-D

**ABOVE** Decorative screens, like this contemporary version, can add a distinct artistic touch. At the same time, one can divide a large room into two smaller spaces, perhaps separating a television-viewing area at one end of the room from a cozy reading corner at the other.

**LEFT** A sure conversation starter, this sculpture begs the question: Which designer would feature it on his runway? Its mix of textures is perfectly suited, too, adding even more visual interest to the neutral scheme.

**ABOVE** Minimal furnishings are intentional in this boy's room, allowing the focal-point wall to command attention. Beach-themed words, simply cut out of plywood and painted, give the room a laid-back attitude.

**LEFT** Atop this mantel, a simple arrangement of greens offsets a diagonally placed antique sickle. But a touch of whimsy keeps it from seeming too serious; a chick figurine on the mantel itself and an illuminated goose on the floor keep things light.

# • mirrors and clocks

Even the smallest decorative mirror can add sparkle to a space, bouncing light back into the room. As a general rule, position a mirror where it will reflect something worth seeing twice, such as a breathtaking view or an eye-catching work of art. Or use an oversize mirror at one end of the room, seemingly doubling the dimensions of the space.

Mirrors can make a strong decorative statement on their own or in a group; you can put together a collection just as you would paintings or prints. For that matter, the same applies to clocks. Used alone, a classic timepiece fitted with chimes can be a strong focal point. On the other hand, a collection of basic round clocks—each set to a different time zone—will clue your guests in on your penchant for travel.

**A collection of mirrors is grouped on one wall of this living room just like pictures or prints. The varied shapes and sizes keep things visually interesting, while the mirrored surfaces bounce light back into the space.**

**ABOVE** Function meets fashion in this dining area, where an oversize wall clock takes on artistic flair, even serving as the focal point of the room.

**BELOW** An exquisite mirror in this master bedroom perfectly completes the dressing area. It's strategically placed, too; you can admire the artwork on the opposite wall even with your back to it.

When it comes to accessorizing a mantel, there is a fail-safe solution: The proverbial picture over the fireplace can still be one of the best options. Before you come to any firm design decisions, though, think about how you can best enhance the architecture of the fireplace and the room as a whole. Do you want to create a soaring sense of height, perhaps in keeping with a cathedral ceiling? Or do you want to keep things more on eye level, creating a horizontal look that echoes the surface of the mantel itself?

There really is no right or wrong answer; it's purely a matter of personal preference. Take some time to play around with different options, keeping in mind that your mantel arrangement will have a more unified look if items placed at the front overlap those in the back.

Though this arrangement starts typically enough, with a pair of prints over the mantel, it's taken to a 3-D level with the addition of a wood bench, topped with precious collectibles that include a vintage typewriter.

# tablescapes

● ● ● THERE'S AN ART TO CREATING A SUCCESSFUL tablescape, one that doesn't overwhelm the display surface. A collection of framed photos, for instance, may be well suited to the top of a console table but too crowded on a smaller end table. It's always a good idea to incorporate a little breathing room into a tablescape; it lets you better appreciate the merits of each piece.

To create a visually pleasing arrangement, use an odd number of items; it will keep things from getting static, encouraging the eye to move from place to place. Start by placing your tallest item at the back and then work your way forward, ending with the smallest piece at the front of the area you're working with. For a well-balanced look, be sure that heights vary—from side to side and front to back. If too many items are similar in height, use small books—or something similar in size and shape—to give them a lift.

**Vintage alarm clocks in staggered sizes are the centerpiece of this tablescape, the twosome doubling their importance. There's a connectivity to the group as a whole, too, as the clocks repeat the predominant black-and-white hues.**

By grouping multiple elements on the tabletop, the eye simply sees it as three. They're not only different in size and shape but also in height, giving movement to the collection.

# ARTISTIC TABLES

Think of the decorative touches in a room, and your mind undoubtedly turns to paintings, prints, and all manner of smaller accessories. But the furniture itself can have an artistic flair. This cocktail table, for example, embellished with calligraphy, is something that you might find in an art gallery.

Don't hesitate, though, to create your own one-of-a-kind piece. A glass-topped table, for instance, provides the perfect opportunity to create a collage beneath its surface. You can use any flat materials, from wine labels to vintage sheet music. Or, if you're crafty, decoupage a wood tabletop with images that reflect your personal style, finishing with a coat of lacquer to preserve your work of art.

With calligraphy scrawled across its top, this unique table would be the perfect addition to an otherwise neutral, understated room; the striking piece creates an instant focal point.

# pillows and bed linens

●●● TO INFUSE A ROOM WITH COLOR AND pattern, sometimes all it takes is a soft touch—in the form of pillows, throws, or bed linens. Plus, they lend themselves to a quick change of scene; a white sofa with pink floral pillows, for instance, can take on a dramatically different look by simply switching the pillows out for black-and-white geometric forms.

Damask pillows may speak to the traditionalist in you, while those with hand-painted covers might reveal your appreciation for art. Like pillows, bed linens are both fashionable and functional. Today's sleeping spots are often decked out in multipatterned layers that can make them the focal point of a room. It's no surprise, really, when you consider the current affinity for eclectic style. Home decor is infinitely more interesting when things mix but don't match.

Inspired by the room's blue-and-white upholstery, bed linens carry out the two-tone theme. While the shades of blue and white are not an exact match, they blend beautifully, which can come off as more casual—and more comforting.

**LEFT** Without the bright orange bed linens, the neutral scheme in this room could have been understated to the point of being sleepy. The lively pop of color, though, establishes the bed as the uncontested focal point of the space.

**ABOVE** Pillows offer one of the easiest and most inexpensive ways to add color and pattern to a room. Case in point is this living room's beach-themed pillows, which quickly establish a fun, easygoing attitude.

**LEFT** A wide variety of textures and patterns—from solid-color linen to lacy eyelet to appliquéd felt hands—appear in this collection of pillows. What makes them all work together, though, are their common-denominator colors.

# collectibles

●●● COLLECTIBLES ARE SOME OF THE BEST candidates for putting a personal stamp on a room. When showcasing collectibles of any kind, be sure that you don't break up the set; pieces grouped together make a more dramatic impact than if they are scattered throughout a room.

Sometimes the collectibles themselves will offer clues as to how to present them best. Items that are graduated in size or color, for instance, have a built-in order. Likewise, if you're a collector of colorful glassware, you might organize it according to the rainbow's spectrum. Whether you have just a few treasured pieces or they appear innumerable, the effect is sure to be striking.

**ABOVE** Wall art teams up with tabletop items in this travel-themed collection. The three-dimensional approach keeps the eye moving from piece to piece, making the collection seem bigger than its actual size.

**RIGHT** Stacks of colorful pottery stand out prominently on the shelves of this country-style pine hutch, making them just as much a finishing touch in this kitchen as they are a functional part of it.

A collection need not be one type of item but, as in this living room, might instead be focused on shape. Everything within these shelves is round, the repetition creating a dramatic effect.

Standard bookshelves in this guest room get volumes more in terms of style. In lieu of the more expected tomes, shelves are filled with favorite collectibles, all with a certain rustic quality.

# more about...
## KIDS' STUFF

Some of the finishing touches you'll hold most dear are items made by your children or things they collected during their growing-up years. You'll probably find them as close as your own storage closets, and the price is right, too. Like any other collectible, they'll make a more dramatic impact if grouped together—on a tabletop, shelf, anywhere they're in plain sight. The result will invariably be a one-of-kind collection that catches the eye and brings a smile.

**ABOVE** A child's paintings, all framed and matted exactly alike, march across the shelves in the family room, providing a welcome variety of color against the all-blue piano and walls.

**ABOVE** Not surprisingly, these quirky collectibles have a wonderful childlike quality; they've been made, through the years, by the owners' daughter.

**BELOW** These colorful vintage lunch boxes would have been eye-catching in their own right but because they're placed on a well-lit ledge, the effect is doubly so.

# photo credits

p. vi: © Eric Roth, design: marthasvineyardinteriordesign.com (top left); © Mark Lohman (top center); © Deborah Whitlaw Lewellyn (top right); © Eric Roth, design: www.capellodesign.com (bottom left); © Tria Giovan (bottom center); © Eric Roth, design: www.webstercompany.com (bottom right)

p. 1: © Mark Lohman (top left); © David Duncan Livingston (top right); © David Duncan Livingston (bottom left); © Mali Azima (bottom right)

p. 2-3: © Hulya Kolabas (left); © Susan Teare, architecture and interior design: Mitra Designs Studio, www.mitradesigns.com (center); © Tria Giovan (right)

## CHAPTER 1

p. 4: © Hulya Kolabas

p. 6: © Eric Roth, design: theodoreandcompany.com

p. 7: © Ryann Ford, design: Roger Hazard, www.rogerandchris.com (top); © Mark Lohman (bottom)

p. 8: © Eric Roth, design: www.kellymonnahan.com

p. 9: © Deborah Whitlaw Lewellyn (top); © Philip Clayton-Thompson, design: Garrison Hullinger Interior Design (bottom left); © Annie Schlechter (bottom right)

p. 10: © Deborah Whitlaw Lewellyn

p. 11: © Eric Roth, design: marthasvineyardinteriordesign.com (top); © Mark Lohman (bottom left); © Ryann Ford, design: Roger Hazard, www.rogerandchris.com (bottom right)

p. 12: © Mark Lohman

pp. ii-iii: © David Duncan Livingston

p. 13: © Ken Gutmaker, design: Bruce Kading Interior Design (top left); © Mark Lohman (top right); © Paul Crosby (bottom)

## CHAPTER 2

p. 14: © Mark Lohman

p. 16: © David Duncan Livingston

p. 17: © Mali Azima (top left); © Mark Lohman (top right); © Eric Roth, design: www.matthewsapera.com (bottom)

p. 18: © David Duncan Livingston

p. 19: © Eric Roth, design: Margo Ouellette (top left); © Deborah Whitlaw Lewellyn (top right); © Eric Roth (bottom)

p. 20: © Mark Lohman

p. 21: © Ryann Ford, design: Kelly Moseley, www.anabelinteriors.com (left); © Jo-Ann Richards, design: Ines Hanl, The Sky is The Limit Design (top right); © Hulya Kolabas, design: Stacey Gendelman Interiors (bottom right)

p. 22: © Ryann Ford

p. 23: © Hulya Kolabas, design: Christina Murphy Interiors (top); © Brian Vanden Brink, design: Breese Architects (bottom left); © Mark Lohman (bottom right)

p. 24: © Ryann Ford, design: Heather Scott Home and Design, www.heatherscotthome.com (top); © Deborah Whitlaw Lewellyn (bottom)

p. 25: © Ken Gutmaker (top); © David Duncan Livingston (bottom)

p. 26: © Mark Lohman

p. 27: © Eric Roth, design: www.lizcaan.com (left); © Mark Lohman (right)

p. 28: © Ryann Ford, design: Roger Hazard, www.rogerandchris.com (top); © Hulya Kolabas, design: Tiffany Eastman Interiors (bottom)

p. 29: © Mark Lohman

p. 30: © Eric Roth, design: www.svdesign.com

p. 31: © Annie Schlechter (top); © David Duncan Livingston (bottom)

p. 32: © Olson Photographic, design: William Earls Architects

p. 33: © Mali Azima (top); © Hulya Kolabas, design: CWB Architects (bottom)

p. 34: © Mark Lohman

p. 35: © Ryann Ford, design: Adam Fortner, www.creativeandsons.com (left); © Mark Lohman (top right); © Eric Roth, design: www.mdcdesignconstruct.com (bottom right)

p. 36: © Annie Schlechter

p. 37: © Susan Teare, architecture and interior design: Mitra Designs Studio, www.mitradesigns.com (top); © Mark Lohman (bottom)

p. 38: © Mark Lohman (left); © Deborah Whitlaw Lewellyn (top right); © Hulya Kolabas (bottom right)

p. 39: © Mali Azima

p. 40: © Mark Lohman (left); © Ryann Ford, design: Jim Poteet, www.poteetarchitects.com (right)

p. 41: © Ryann Ford, design: Kelly Moseley, www.anabelinteriors.com (top); © Mark Lohman (bottom)

## CHAPTER 3

p. 42: © Deborah Whitlaw Lewellyn

p. 44: © Eric Roth, design: www.capellodesign.com

p. 45: © Deborah Whitlaw Lewellyn (top); © Eric Roth, design: www.jninteriorspaces.com (bottom)

p. 46: © Eric Roth, design: marthasvineyardinteriordesign.com

p. 47: © Tria Giovan (top); © Eric Roth, design: www.hutkerarchitects.com (bottom)

p. 48: © Eric Roth, design: www.lauriegorelickinteriors.com

p. 49: © Deborah Whitlaw Lewellyn (top left); © Mark Lohman (top right); © Mali Azima (bottom)

p. 50: © Tria Giovan

p. 51: © Tria Giovan (top); © Eric Roth, design: marthasvineyardinteriordesign.com (bottom left); © Hulya Kolabas, design: CWB Architects (bottom right)

p. 52: © Deborah Whitlaw Lewellyn (left); © Hulya Kolabas (right)

p. 53: © David Duncan Livingston (top); © David Duncan Livingston (bottom)

p. 54: © David Duncan Livingston

p. 55: © Hulya Kolabas (top); © Mali Azima (center); Courtesy of La-Z-Boy (bottom)

p. 56: © Mark Lohman (top); © Deborah Whitlaw Lewellyn (bottom)

p. 57: © Mali Azima

p. 58: © Olson Photographic, design: VAS Construction (top); © Mali Azima (bottom)

p. 59: © Eric Roth, design: www.lizcaan.com (left); © Deborah Whitlaw Lewellyn (right)

p. 60: © Annie Schlechter

p. 61: © Brian Vanden Brink, design: The Green Company (top left); © Ryann Ford, design: Kimberly Renner, www.therennerproject.com (top right); © Deborah Whitlaw Lewellyn (bottom left); © Mali Azima (bottom right)

p. 62: © Ken Gutmaker, design: Shannon Del Vecchio

p. 63: © Deborah Whitlaw Lewellyn (top); © Eric Roth, design: Carol Sarason Design (bottom)

p. 64: © Eric Roth, design: Kevin Thomas Interior Design (left); © Eric Roth, design: Carol Sarason Design (right)

p. 65: © Tria Giovan

p. 66: © Hulya Kolabas (top); © Laurie Black, design: Amy Baker Interior Design, Seattle, WA (bottom)

p. 67: © Tria Giovan

p. 68: © Philip Clayton-Thompson, design: Garrison Hullinger Interior Design

p. 69: © Hulya Kolabas, design: Susan Glick Interiors (top left); © Mali Azima (bottom left); © David Duncan Livingston (right)

p. 70: © Hulya Kolabas, design: Tiffany Eastman Interiors (top); © Deborah Whitlaw Lewellyn (bottom)

p. 71: © Philip Clayton-Thompson, design: Garrison Hullinger Interior Design (top); © Eric Roth, design: www.feinmann.com (bottom)

p. 72: © Eric Roth

p. 73: © David Duncan Livingston (top left); © Mali Azima (bottom left); © Hulya Kolabas, design: Joanna Heimbold (right)

p. 74: © Mali Azima (left); © David Duncan Livingston (right)

p. 75: © Eric Roth (left); © Eric Roth, design: www.jninteriorspaces.com (right)

p. 76: © Hulya Kolabas, design: Christina Murphy Interiors

p. 77: © Ryann Ford, design: Heather Scott Home and Design, www.heatherscotthome.com (top left); © Eric Roth, design: fdhodgeinteriors.com (top right); © Eric Roth, design: adamsbeasley.com (bottom)

p. 78: © Eric Roth, design: danielhreynolds.com (left); © Eric Roth, design: www.kellymcguillhome.com (right)

p. 79: © Mark Lohman

p. 80: © Mark Lohman (top); © Mark Lohman (bottom)

p. 81: © Annie Schlechter (top); © Mali Azima (bottom)

p. 82: © Hulya Kolabas, design: Stacey Gendelman Interiors

p. 83: © Eric Roth, design: www.jninteriorspaces.com (top); © Jo-Ann Richards, design: Ivan Meade, Meade Design Group (bottom)

p. 84: © Eric Roth, design: www.kellymcguillhome.com (top); © David Duncan Livingston (bottom left); © Deborah Whitlaw Lewellyn (bottom right)

p. 85: © Annie Schlechter (top); © Mark Lohman (bottom left); © Annie Schlechter (bottom right)

## CHAPTER 4

p. 86: © Tria Giovan

p. 88: © David Duncan Livingston, design: Scheinholtz Associates, schein@pacbell.net (top); © David Duncan Livingston, design: Scheinholtz Associates, schein@pacbell.net (bottom)

p. 89: © David Duncan Livingston, design: Scheinholtz Associates, schein@pacbell.net

p. 90: © Hulya Kolabas

p. 91: © Eric Roth, design: adamsbeasley.com (top); © Eric Roth (bottom)

p. 92: © Chipper Hatter

p. 93: © Hulya Kolabas (top); © Olson Photographic, design: Stacey Gendelman Designs (bottom)

p. 94: © Eric Roth, design: www.capellodesign.com

p. 95: © Hulya Kolabas (top); © Brian Vanden Brink, design: Polhemus Savery DaSilva Architects Builders (bottom left); © Mali Azima (bottom right)

p. 97: © David Duncan Livingston (top); © David Duncan Livingston (bottom left); © Hulya Kolabas, design: Christina Murphy Interiors (bottom right)

p. 98: © Susan Teare, design: Peregrine Design/Build, architect: Stephen Wanta

p. 99: © Mark Lohman (top); © Mark Lohman (bottom left); © Eric Roth, design: www.fbnconstruction.com (bottom right)

p. 100: Eric Roth, design: marthasvineyardinteriordesign.com

p. 101: © Brian Vanden Brink, design: Sally Weston, Architect (top); © Ryann Ford (bottom)

## CHAPTER 5

p. 102: © Tria Giovan

p. 104: © Mali Azima

p. 105: © Olson Photographic, design: InnerSpace Electronics, Inc. (top); © David Duncan Livingston (bottom)

p. 106: © Mark Lohman

p. 107: © Eric Roth, design: theodoreandcompany.com (left); © Deborah Whitlaw Lewellyn (right)

p. 108: © David Duncan Livingston

p. 109: © Eric Roth, design: The Lagasse Group (top); © Eric Roth, design: www.georgiazikasdesign.com (bottom left); © Eric Roth, design: www.matthewsapera.com (bottom right)

p. 110: © Hulya Kolabas

p. 111: © Eric Roth (top); © Eric Roth, design: www.kellymonnahan.com (bottom left); © Deborah Whitlaw Lewellyn (bottom right)

p. 112: © Hulya Kolabas, design: Stacey Gendelman Interiors (left); © Mark Lohman (right)

p. 113: © Deborah Whitlaw Lewellyn (left); © Mark Lohman (right)

p. 114: © Eric Roth, design: www.catherineandmcclure.com

p. 115: © Eric Roth, design: www.mdcdesignconstruct.com (top left); © Brian Vanden Brink, design: Phi Home Design (top right); © Eric Roth, design: www.catherineandmcclure.com (bottom)

p. 116: © Tria Giovan (top); © Mark Lohman (bottom)

p. 117: © Eric Roth, design: www.mdcdesignconstruct.com

p. 118: © Eric Roth, design: www.psdab.com (top); © Philip Clayton-Thompson, design: Garrison Hullinger Interior Design (bottom)

p. 119: © Mark Lohman (top); © Mark Lohman (bottom)

p. 120: © Mali Azima

p. 121: © Mark Lohman (top left); © Hulya Kolabas, design: Joanna Heimbold (top right); © Chipper Hatter (bottom)

## CHAPTER 6

p. 122: © Hulya Kolabas

p. 124: © Mark Lohman

p. 125: © Mark Lohman (top); © Eric Roth (bottom)

p. 126: © Annie Schlechter (top); © Annie Schlechter (bottom)

p. 127: © Olson Photographic, design: Jonathan Butler Architects (left); © Deborah Whitlaw Lewellyn (right)

p. 128: © Eric Roth, design: www.webstercompany.com

p. 129: © David Duncan Livingston (top); © Deborah Whitlaw Lewellyn (bottom left); © Hulya Kolabas (bottom right)

p. 130: © Hulya Kolabas (top); © Deborah Whitlaw Lewellyn (bottom)

p. 131: © Annie Schlechter (top); © Annie Schlechter (bottom left); © Annie Schlechter (bottom right)

p. 132: © Mark Lohman (left); © Mark Lohman (right)

p. 133: © Laurie Black, design: Hyde Evans Design, Seattle, WA

p. 134: © Tria Giovan

p. 135: © Philip Clayton-Thompson, design: Garrison Hullinger Interior Design (top); © Brian Vanden Brink, design: Group 3 (bottom)

p. 136: © Brian Vanden Brink, design: Houses & Barns by John Libby (top); © Mali Azima (bottom)

p. 137: © Philip Clayton-Thompson, design: Garrison Hullinger Interior Design (top); © Philip Clayton-Thompson, design: Garrison Hullinger Interior Design (bottom)

p. 138: © Chipper Hatter (left); © Eric Roth, design: Margo Ouellette (right)

p. 139: © Annie Schlechter

p. 140: © David Duncan Livingston

p. 141: © Chipper Hatter (top left); © Annie Schlechter (top right); © Mark Lohman (bottom left); © Jo-Ann Richards, design: Lorin Turner, Zebra Group (bottom right)

p. 142: © Brian Vanden Brink, design: Siemasko & Verbridge Architects (top); © Jo-Ann Richards, design: Ines Hanl, The Sky is The Limit Design (bottom)

p. 143: Mark Lohman (top); © Susan Teare, design: Peregrine Design/Build (bottom)

p. 144: © Brian Vanden Brink, design: Group 3 (left); © Eric Roth (right)

p. 145: © Eric Roth, design: Carol Sarason Design

## CHAPTER 7

p. 146: © Hulya Kolabas

p. 148: © David Duncan Livingston (left); © Mark Lohman (right)

p. 149: © Eric Roth, design: www.gleysteendesign.com (top); © Mark Lohman (bottom)

p. 150: © Eric Roth

p. 151: © Chipper Hatter (top); © Eric Roth (bottom)

p. 152: © David Duncan Livingston

p. 153: © Brian Vanden Brink, design: Catalano Architects (top left); © Eric Roth (top right); © Eric Roth, design: www.benjaminnutter.com (bottom left); © Eric

Roth, design: www.benjaminnutter.com (bottom right)

p. 154: © Eric Roth, design: www.marcyephilbrook.com (top); © Eric Roth (bottom)

p. 155: © Tria Giovan

p. 156: © Mark Lohman (left); © Eric Roth, design: marthasvineyardinteriordesign.com (right)

p. 157: © Eric Roth, design: www.matthewsapera.com

p. 158: © Hulya Kolabas

p. 159: © Brian Vanden Brink, design: Hope Angier (top); © Eric Roth (bottom left); © Eric Roth, design: www.nicoleyee.com (bottom center); © Eric Roth, design: marthasvineyardinteriordesign.com (bottom right)

p. 160: Charles Miller © The Taunton Press (left); © Mark Lohman (right)

p. 161: © Mark Lohman

p. 162: © Eric Roth, design: www.pamelacopeman.com

p. 163: © Susan Teare, design: Peregrine Design/Build, architect: Ernie Ruskey (left); © Eric Roth, design: www.jninteriorspaces.com (right)

p. 164: © Hulya Kolabas (left); © David Duncan Livingston (right)

p. 165: © Brian Vanden Brink

p. 166: © Eric Roth, design: www.svdesign.com (left); © Deborah Whitlaw Lewellyn (right)

p. 167: © David Duncan Livingston (left); © Eric Roth, design: www.catherineandmcclure.com (right)

## CHAPTER 8

p. 168: © Brian Vanden Brink, design: Group 3

p. 170: © Eric Roth, design: treehousedesigninc.com (left); © Brian Vanden Brink (right)

p. 171: © Deborah Whitlaw Lewellyn (left); © Olson Photographic, design: Bartels-Pagliaro Architects (right)

p. 172: © Mali Azima

p. 173: © Mali Azima (top); © Hulya Kolabas, design: CWB Architects (bottom left); © Chipper Hatter (bottom right)

p. 174: © Eric Roth (top); © Mali Azima (bottom)

p. 175: © Hulya Kolabas, design: Joanna Heimbold (left); © Mali Azima (top right); © Eric Roth, design: bkarch.com (bottom right)

p. 176: © Mali Azima

p. 177: © Hulya Kolabas, design: Lorrie Abonoventura Interiors (top left); © Eric Roth, design: www.jninteriorspaces.com (bottom left); © Hulya Kolabas (right)

p. 178: © Mark Lohman

p. 179: © Mali Azima (left); © Mark Lohman (right)

p. 180: © Tria Giovan

p. 181: © Eric Roth, design: www.kellymcguillhome.com (left); © Tria Giovan (top right); © Eric Roth, design: www.capellodesign.com (bottom right)

p. 182: © David Duncan Livingston

p. 183: © Mark Lohman (left); © Tria Giovan (right)

p. 184: © Eric Roth, design: daherinteriordesign.com

p. 185: © Brian Vanden Brink, design: Hans Warner, architect (top left); © Tria Giovan (top right); © Paul Crosby (bottom left); © Mark Lohman (bottom right)

p. 186: © Brian Vanden Brink, design: Polhemus Savery DaSilva Architects Builders

p. 187: © David Duncan Livingston (top); © Eric Roth (bottom)

p. 188: © Ryann Ford

p. 189: © Mark Lohman (left); © Mark Lohman (top right); © Eric Roth (bottom right)

p. 190: © Mark Lohman

p. 191: © Jo-Ann Richards, design: Lorin Turner, Zebra Group (top); © Eric Roth, design: www.matthewsapera.com (bottom)

p. 192: © Mark Lohman

p. 193: © Mark Lohman (left); © David Duncan Livingston (top right); © Jo-Ann Richards, design: Ines Hanl, The Sky is The Limit Design (bottom right)

p. 194: © Eric Roth, design: www.skaala.us

p. 195: © Eric Roth, design: www.matthewsapera.com (top); © Jo-Ann Richards, design: Ines Hanl, The Sky is The Limit Design (bottom left); © Jo-Ann Richards, design: Ines Hanl, The Sky is The Limit Design (bottom right)

p. 196: © Mark Lohman

p. 197: © David Duncan Livingston (top); © Mark Lohman (bottom left); © Mark Lohman (bottom right)

## CHAPTER 9

p. 198: © Eric Roth, design: www.feinmann.com

p. 200: © Mark Lohman

p. 201: © Brian Vanden Brink, design: Polhemus Savery DaSilva Architects Builders (left); © David Duncan Livingston (right)

p. 202: © Tria Giovan (top); © Mark Lohman (bottom)

p. 203: © David Duncan Livingston (top); © Annie Schlechter (bottom)

p. 204: © David Duncan Livingston

p. 205: © David Duncan Livingston (top left); © Ryann Ford, design: Heather Scott Home and Design, www.heatherscotthome.com (top right); © Eric Roth, design: daherinteriordesign.com (bottom left); © Ken Gutmaker (bottom right)

p. 206: © Brian Vanden Brink, design: Hutker Architects (left); © Eric Roth, design: www.lauriegorelickinteriors.com (right)

p. 207: © Deborah Whitlaw Lewellyn (top); © Deborah Whitlaw Lewellyn (bottom)

p. 208: © Hulya Kolabas, design: Mar Silver Design

p. 209: © Deborah Whitlaw Lewellyn (top left); © Deborah Whitlaw Lewellyn (bottom left); © Mali Azima (right)

p. 210: © Brian Vanden Brink, design: Catalano Architects

p. 211: © Ken Gutmaker, design: Shannon Del Vecchio (left); © Eric Roth, design: duncanhughes.com (right)

p. 212: © Mark Lohman

p. 213: © Deborah Whitlaw Lewellyn (top); © Eric Roth, design: www.jonathancutlerarchitect.com (bottom)

## CHAPTER 10

p. 214: © Chipper Hatter

p. 216: © Hulya Kolabas, design: Mar Silver Design (left); © Eric Roth (right)

p. 217: © Mark Lohman (top); © Mali Azima (bottom)

p. 218: © Ryann Ford

p. 219: © Mark Lohman (top); © Deborah Whitlaw Lewellyn (bottom)

p. 220: © Eric Roth, design: duncanhughes.com

p. 221: © Eric Roth, design: Margo Ouellette (top left); © Mali Azima (top right); © Deborah Whitlaw Lewellyn (bottom left); © Tria Giovan (bottom right)

p. 222: © David Duncan Livingston

p. 223: © Eric Roth, design: daherinteriordesign.com (top left); © Mali Azima (bottom left); © Ryann Ford, design: Mari Johnson, www.backhomeliving.com (right)

p. 224: © Eric Roth, design: www.kellymcguillhome.com

p. 225: © Hulya Kolabas, design: Tiffany Eastman Interiors (left); © Mali Azima (right)

p. 226: © Hulya Kolabas

p. 227: © Stacy Bass, design: Allison Caccoma, Caccoma Interiors (top left); © Mali Azima (bottom left); © Ken Gutmaker (right)

p. 228: © Ryann Ford (left); © Tria Giovan (right)

p. 229: © Mali Azima

p. 230: © Mali Azima

p. 231: © Deborah Whitlaw Lewellyn (top left); © Annie Schlechter (top right); © Eric Roth, design: www.meichipeng.com (bottom)